Another collection
from Neil H

Fortress H:

The Teenage Years

Eastern Daily Press

Copyright 2000 Eastern Counties Newspapers

Published by Eastern Counties Newspapers, Prospect House, Rouen Road, Norwich, Norfolk NR1 1RE.

Printed and bound by Page Bros, Mile Cross Lane, Norwich.

ISBN 1-902729-05-6

Produced by Gavin Davies

Photography by Simon Lunt

In loving memory of Dad

Contents

FOREWORD

Someone said to me recently: "Don't you mind having your secrets in the paper every week?"

Well, to be honest, after ten years it's a bit too late for that. I suppose in the early days I did wonder whether it was a good idea. Especially when people started making odd remarks to me in the village. But as time has gone by, the sympathy vote seems to be more with me than Neil - and so it should be.

He makes out how hard done by he is but if you read between the lines, you realise he doesn't have it so bad. If you bump into him the street, just take a look at him. You will immediately spot that he is well fed - probably a bit too well. And no, he doesn't live on a diet of Aubergine Bake.

And remind him that the beer fairy makes sure supplies of his favourite tipple are always available.

Ask him when he last ironed one of his shirts. On the rare occasion when he does it's usually more creased than when he started.

I suppose there is one well-kept secret - and that's me. Most of you don't know what I look like. True you may have formed an impression from my husband's ramblings but the real me is something even Neil has managed to keep a secret.

He delights in telling everyone the story of the time we were with a group of people at a function. A couple approached him and asked which one of the females was Mrs H.

I happened to be chatting to a friend at the time and Neil had great pleasure in pointing to me saying: "Can't you tell? She's the one doing all the talking."

With this the lady moved closer to him and whispered: "Do you know, I expected a much bigger woman."

Well, let me state once and for all, I am not big, neither am I a monster. All right, people that know me do say: "Your husband's got you off to a T!" So I suppose I have to concede that maybe there is a grain of truth in what he writes.

But imagine what it's like living with someone whose motto is: "Never do today what you can put off until tomorrow"?

And if you're having trouble with that, just read this book - but do read between the lines!

Mrs H

CAUGHT IN THE CROSSFIRE
OF A BRAT BATTLE

I've become more aware recently of the number of people who have said to me: "It only gets worse". They are referring to the traumatic role of parenting. "You wait. Even when they leave home they still think you're a bottomless pit of money."

I think I'm more sensitive to these comments because Brat Major is now a teenager and has assumed that typical look. The nose in the air, the clenched lips and the defiant jaw, eyes that burn into you when something is denied.

She is a great mutterer. She mumbles away as if she is holding a conversation and I sometimes wonder if there is someone else living with us. Having been sent to do something which she feels is a violation of her rights she mooches off jabbering to herself. Out of sheer curiosity the other day I crept after her and listened to her rantings.

"I'll change my T-shirt if she says I have to. But I don't see why I should. It's my T-shirt and it's my life. Nobody else has to change their T-shirt just because their mother tells them to." I suppose it helps her let off steam.

The other thing I've noticed recently is that they squabble more than they used to. They always have argued but it seems to be more physical now. Hand to hand inter-brat combat is sparked off by almost anything, from how loud the TV is to whether the last piece of chocolate cake has been divided equally in two portions.

The other night, Brat Minor was stretching to reach his toothbrush from the bathroom cabinet when his sister happened upon him. Playfully, or so she insists, she dug him in the ribs. The startled young gentleman yelped with surprise, dropped the toothbrush and hit the deck.

In retaliation he aimed a wild kick at Brat Major. She took a pace to the left and he buried his foot painfully into the bathroom door. Humiliated at being so embarrassingly out-manoeuvred, he went for the kill and I had to prise them apart.

These battles always follow the same pattern. The recipient of the first blow will screech in pain regardless of the severity of the injury sustained. The object is to alert a parent who will immediately side with the casualty and impose swingeing punishment on the enemy.

We are, of course, wise to this. Providing there is no evidence of a need to call the emergency services, we go for the easiest solution. Apportion blame equally and issue each with the same punishment. All this guerrilla warfare means that Mrs H and I are forever intervening in some dispute or other. Only the other day I attended a typical skirmish.

There was a thump followed by a piercing howl of pain from Brat Minor. At the very least he must have lost a limb. I arrived on the scene to be greeted by his lordship rubbing his head.

"She opened the front door and hit my head," he wailed. The teenager began to protest her innocence. But we no longer bother to hear the case, consider the evidence and arrive at a verdict. We go straight to passing the sentence. I sucked in a suitable supply of oxygen.

"Both of you in your rooms NOW!"

"But..but.."

"I don't want to hear it. Get up there and you won't come out until I say so." There, that's told 'em. What we need round here is a bit of discipline.

I have since learnt that Brat Major had opened the front door as their friend from up the road had called. Unbeknown to me he was still the other side of the door when I let fly. Hearing my outburst he swiftly put as much distance as possible between him and Fortress H. Later he confided in my daughter: "I didn't know your father could shout like that. I always thought he was so mellow."

Having an independent witness to my display of authority could have gone some way to dispelling my reputation as being a pussy cat in comparison to Mrs H but for one thing. I was completely in the wrong. Brat Major had flung open the door to greet their chum. Brat Minor in his enthusiasm to get to the door had simply got in the way and, quite accidentally, received a clout on the head.

Within minutes of retiring to their rooms they bravely came down to lodge an appeal. The fact that they were in agreement with each other indicated they must be in the right. I was forced to climb down in front of a sniggering Mrs H.

I stomped off grumbling. "I can't stand much more of this. They're bad enough now. What ever is it going to be like when they get worse?"

"Careful," Mrs H called after me. "You're muttering."

JUST KNOT
GOOD ENOUGH

You can tell when Mrs H is approaching meltdown. First there is the widening of the eyes. Then the mouth opens to take additional oxygen on board so the ensuing verbals can be delivered without losing momentum through pausing for breath.

Most of the time I can spot it and immediately slip into my metaphoric asbestos suit. The younger inmates of Fortress Haverson have not yet honed their antennae to tune in to the approaching shock waves so they suffer the consequences. Brat Minor was the victim the other day as he was attempting to liberate some fruit juice from the fridge.

"Look out!" yelled Mrs H. As he tugged the container off the shelf he nudged an apple which rolled gently out of the fridge and bounced across the floor. "It'll be bruised now," she complained. Brat Minor looked at his mother, failed to spot the warning signs, retrieved the apple and put it back in the fridge. He then made his fatal mistake.

He lunged for the juice once more and, of course, he again caught the apple. It repeated its bruising journey across the kitchen floor, landing at Mrs H's feet. Meltdown was upgraded to ballistic.

"How many time do I have to tell you two the same things!" she exploded. "It wouldn't matter if I told you things a thousand times- no a hundred thousand times. You still wouldn't listen!" Brat Minor grabbed the apple and replaced it. The whole sequence of events would have been repeated yet again if Mrs H hadn't guided him through the exercise.

At least when they are babies you have a certain amount of control. Yes, they do keep you awake at night. And they have you cleaning up food which has been recycled and ejected from which ever end will cause maximum disruption at the time. However, they don't answer back and are totally reliant upon you for transport.

By the time they hit double figures you can feel your grip on them loosening by the day. Eventually you are clinging on by your fingertips awaiting the inevitable drop over the precipice into the abyss of anarchy.

I have just received confirmation that I have finally lost control. It came while I was attempting to assert myself the other night. Brat Major was engaging me in a bout of sparring as I was attempting to get her up to bed. She will persist with this protest that her wicked parents leave her disadvantaged. Her schoolmates, she insists, are allowed to stay up into the early hours of the morning watching television while she is made to go to bed at a reasonable time.

Anyway, on this particular evening I had had enough of her prevaricating. "Will you get up those stairs NOW!" I shouted in my best I'm the boss voice. She leaned forward and cupped my face in both her hands.

"You're lovely when you get angry Dad." There wasn't much I could say after that. So much for my authority.

It was the Queen's recent visit to Norwich that really put my position in perspective. Brat Minor was asking his mother what the Queen's role is. She told him that the Queen has no real powers. The government runs the country. It is just a formality that the Queen gives her Royal Assent to Bills. This all sounded rather familiar and I was able to give my son a simple analogy.

"It's rather like me," I explained. "I am supposed to be head of the household but I just do as I'm told like the rest of you." In fact my role differs from that of the Queen. At least Parliament waits for her to sign on the dotted line before the bill goes on to the statute book. Mrs H has been known to implement new regulations without any prior notice whatsoever.

At least I shall be well prepared when Great Britain finally becomes just a colony of Europe and we loose control of our own destiny. Fortress Haverson has been operating along these lines for years. I huff and puff importantly but in truth I have very little clout.

If I apprehend a Brat with its finger in the biscuit tin I will admonish said Brat and impose a sentence of say an hour's confinement to the bedroom. If the Fortress Court of Justice in the form of Mrs H gets to hear about it there is every chance the punishment will be overturned and quite possibly increased.

And then we have Mrs H's common agricultural policy. She sets the quotas for what we grow and I do the work. We already have a common currency. It's called my salary.

I don't have the power of veto so there's no point in fighting any of it. I don't know though. Perhaps I'd wheedle my way into her affections more if I put my parts on - since I'm lovely when I'm angry.

TIME FLIES IN THE BRAT-FREE ZONE

I arrived home from work at about twenty past six last Friday evening. It had been a hard week and my head felt as though someone had drilled a hole in it and inserted a wad of cotton wool. I sought out Mrs H. No, I don't know why either. I had no expectations of any sympathy for my condition. But for once she had words of cheer for me.

"Do you realise," she said very deliberately, "he is being picked up for Youth Club at ten to seven and she is off to a birthday disco? He won't be back until half past nine" It took a second or two for the significance of this to sink in.

"You mean...we've got over two hours to ourselves?" By now my thoughts had crystallised and I was able to make a cogent and profound statement. "We can go up the pub!"

Usually, if they're both out together, sod's law says their activities never start and finish at the same time. We spend half the night driving round the village delivering and collecting them. On this occasion, all I had to do was collect Brat Major from her disco - and not until ten o'clock. I was like a dog that has suddenly remembered where he buried a juicy bone.

Brat Major was gone by 6.30. At 6.50 p.m. his lordship was seen off the premises and we entered the Brat-free Zone. Fuelled by optimism, I had long since jettisoned the cotton wool from my addled brain. But I hadn't allowed for Mrs H getting ready. She was shifting into ball gown mode. The meter was running.

6.51 p.m. Mrs H announces that her skirt has got a crease and will need ironing. "Your jumper could do with a press too. Get the ironing board out and I'll do them when I've got ready."

6.53 p.m. Bath taps turned on. I release impatient sigh. "All right, all right I'll be quick," replied Mrs H testily.

6.55 p.m. Bathroom door opens. "Can you plug my hot brush in for me? I haven't got any clothes on." What difference does that make? Does nakedness induce electric shocks?

7.12 p.m. Bathroom ominously silent. I crash in. "All right, I'm getting out! Relaxing in the bath is all part of going out." Yes but time is ticking away. I knew better than to voice those thoughts.

7.20 p.m. We are thirty minutes into our Brat-free time. I am putting on my shirt. "Your deodorant has dried quickly," observed Mrs H, "I used the spray. If I'd used the roll-on, we'd still be here at eight o'clock. Probably still will be at this rate." Oops!

As soon as I said it I knew I was wrong.

"We don't have to go out if you're going to be like that," came the terse reply.

7.25 p.m. "Oh No! My daughter's pinched my best tights. I'll have to look for another pair." More valuable time gone.

7.30 p.m. Mrs H begins ironing.

7.35 p.m. "Oh Neil. The sky is black. It looks like rain. Could you just get the towels off the washing line." Aaarrgggh!

7.40 p.m. Make up being adjusted. I'm pacing the hall.

7.45 p.m. Bedroom door closes. Yes! This must be it.

7.45.30 p.m. Bedroom door reopens. Chosen jacket will not fit over chosen jumper.

7.50 p.m. "Right. I must just try on my new shoes." Hall carpet showing signs of wear.

7.52 p.m. Mrs H arrives in hall. "Hang on. I must just take some things out of my handbag. It's so full."

7.53 p.m. Yes! Yes! The front door is opening. We're off...oh no we're not. Mrs H re-enters house giggling. "Look. I've still got the labels on the soles of my new shoes."

7.54 p.m. We're in the car. Mrs H plays her trump card. "You have got some money haven't you?" Curses. I put my wallet down while I was pacing the hall. "It's a good job I've got some then isn't it?" She can be really smug when she wants to.

8 p.m. At last! We're in the pub. One hour plus of our Brat-free time has already elapsed. Suddenly it's past 9.05 p.m. Our brief encounter with the luxury of being just a couple again has passed.

9.22 p.m. We're home. It hasn't rained so Mrs H steps into the night to hang out more washing. Normality has returned to Fortress Haverson.

9.40 p.m. A whirlwind enters the house in the form of Brat Minor and I am dispatched to collect Brat Major from her disco at 10 p.m.

10.10 p.m. The disco is running late. Having earlier paced the Fortress Hall I am now pacing the Village Hall.

Evenings of freedom like this come to pass about as often as Halley's Comet and I spent a good third of it at the beck and call of the female members of the family.

Not much different from a normal evening really.

MISSING BRAT ALERT
BRINGS WAVE OF PANIC

It seemed unfair at half term that I had to get up to go to work while the rest of the inmates of Fortress H had a lie-in. In fact, this was most agreeable. The bathroom ceased to be like Piccadilly Circus and I could enjoy a peaceful breakfast.

But on the Wednesday I was awoken early by a couple of bumps. What are they up to now? I thought. I turned over to doze for a bit longer. I opened one eye and looked at the clock. Immediately I was fully awake. It was past 7 a.m. and the buzzer hadn't gone. Must have forgotten to set the alarm. Panic.

As I rushed downstairs I noticed Brat Major's door was open. Ah, I thought, that explains the bumps. The little monkey has got up early. Probably just as well or I would have overslept. Let me see now. She will either be scavenging food or watching television.

But there was no sign of her in the kitchen or the North Wing. Must be in the loo. No, not there either. I was becoming a bit concerned. I checked the rest of the house but she was nowhere to be found. Then I noticed the back door was ajar. What was going on?

My concern was deepening. I returned to her bedroom for a closer inspection. Her pyjamas were there, abandoned on the floor. Clearly she had dressed and gone out. I could feel the onset of a cold sweat. Had she done a runner? The previous evening she had been her normal surly teenage self and indulged in the usual acrimonious sparring with her mother.

"Why can't you be civil to me? Just look at your face. What have I done to deserve this?" Mrs H had implored as Brat Major muttered and scowled. Perhaps she had taken the hump and gone to seek a better life elsewhere.

Then I remembered that, as they were going to bed, there had been some conspiracy between the two younger inmates. They were plotting in Brat Minor's bedroom. I had gone to investigate but been sent packing.

"Get out Dad," Brat Major had ordered. "I'm doing a deal with him." Remembering this I rushed into Brat Minor's bedroom to interrogate the other member of the escape committee. I shook him roughly awake.

"Do you know where your sister is?" I demanded. "What's she up to? I can't find her." He protested that she had not confided in him. I was beginning to feel desperate now. I decided there was nothing for it but to alert the Camp Commandant.

I have never seen Mrs H come to so rapidly. I blurted out that her daughter had legged it and she became conscious in a trice. Together we checked Brat Major's bedroom yet again. Her bag and handbag were still here so she hadn't taken anything. Back to Brat Minor for a further inquisition.

"This is serious," I informed him trying hard to keep the note of hysteria out of my voice. "Your sister has disappeared. What were you two hatching last night."

"Oh that," he said with a distinct lack of concern. "She was offering to clean my bedroom if I gave her some of my pocket money." Mrs H took over.

"You dress properly and drive round the village," she instructed me before turning back to her son to conduct a further interview.

Fuelled by a mixture of fear and panic, I fumbled my way into some clothes. My brain went into hyper-overdrive. Thoughts came tumbling out. This can't be happening to us. It happens to other people. Must 'phone work. Tell them I'll be late. I'll kill her. How soon do we let the police know? Wait till I get my hands on her. No, mustn't be angry with her. Have to appeal on the radio. I can see the headlines "Distraught parents appeal to daughter to come home. Mother says 'She can be petulant if she likes I just want her back.'"

The adrenaline was flowing like Niagara as I pummelled downstairs to grab the car keys. Then I heard footsteps and the back door burst open.

"Next door's rabbits have escaped. I've been trying to catch them. I saw them from my bedroom window." It was a breathless Brat Major quite unaware of the fact that her parents were about to carry out a sweep of the village, run off handbills and commence door-to-door inquiries.

With the drama over I climbed into the bath. What was that noise? Just my heart trying to escape from my chest. Now calm down. How stupid can you get? She wouldn't run away. Not our little girl - would she?

When I got to work I recounted the saga. Those with older children nodded sagely and said oh yes, they had been there. And then they uttered those dreaded words. "Of course you know. It only gets worse."

YES THERE ARE STILL
TIMES WHEN I'M A HERO

I know I complain but Fortress Haverson is indeed blessed to have Mrs H at the helm. She steers the Fortress ship through the choppiest of waters. I rarely venture onto the bridge. I am happier down below, swabbing the decks. Besides, when circumstances do force me into the captain's role invariably I give the wheel a spin the wrong way.

My navigational failings usually occur when one of the ratings fires in a demand which needs an instant decision. I dread it when one of them is on the phone and I hear those loaded words: "I should think it will be all right. I'll just ask Dad. Dad? Can I go round to Janet's?"

Whilst Mrs H seems to haunt me most of the time, it's a dead cert she won't be around when I need her. Anyway, my authority is pretty low at the best of times so it doesn't help if I keep using the old cop out: "I don't know. You'll have to ask your mother." There are times when I must go it alone.

First question; is Janet on the approved list? As I have never had access to the full list, I'm on a loser here if I am not familiar with the caller. Next task is to elicit from the appropriate Brat how time at the friends will be spent. Is what they intend to do on the list of permitted activities?

Once all known criteria have been met, we are at the stage where I would normally become involved. Providing transport. You can bet your life that as we are heading for the car Mrs H will mysteriously appear and want to know what's going on. She then goes through the same questions that I have. The only difference is she knows what the correct answers should be.

But it's in a crisis where Mrs H takes real control. Like the occasion when Brat Major, probably less than two years old at the time, got some curtain wire stuck in her throat. I could not shift it so Mrs H took over. I was dispatched to the phone, where, driven by panic, I tried to ring everyone from the doctor to the TV repairman. Meanwhile Mrs H calmly removed the wire and organised a trip to Casualty.

There is just the one tiny area where I come into my own. It provides my only opportunity to write in this column of my acts of heroism. Yes, it is the capture and ejection of the eight-legged invaders. But there was an incident the other day when I was not at home and a spider set up camp in the north wing. My fellow inmates went to pieces.

Mrs H recounted the tale to me lacing it with colour and drama as only she can. Brat Major produced an actual size drawing of the intruder. It looked like one of those enormous suns she used to draw at playgroup. In fact, so graphic were the descriptions that I formed the impression its diet consisted of nothing smaller than a frog - and that just for a snack. So how did they deal with it?

First, apparently, there was an hysterical conference. Out of this came Mrs H's suggestion that they whack a box over it and leave it until "your father gets home". However, the cunning insect was in a place where a box was unwhackable.

"Ben next door likes spiders," suggested Brat Major referring to the 8-year old who lives in the corner. Mrs H seized on the solution.

"Get him, get him!" she begged.

"I can't. They've gone out for the day."

Then someone suggested Lee who lives at the top of the road.

"Ring him up," pleaded Mrs H. They stood guard over the spider awaiting Lee's arrival. Our hero came into view. A knight on a white charger wielding his sword? No, a thirteen year-old boy sporting goalkeeper's gloves.

There followed a game of cat and mouse before Lee finally trapped the spider. He was instructed to take it a good distance from the house before letting it go. Watched by a trio of grateful Haversons, he went some way up the road and made to release his captive.

"Further, further!" they yelled. This was repeated a number of times until the poor lad was fast becoming a dot on the horizon. Eventually he was given the all clear and the spider was last seen airborne as it was jettisoned over somebody's hedge to inflict further panic on another unsuspecting family.

To show her gratitude Mrs H went to the local bakers and bought the gallant Lee a large cream cake. In fact, presumably to help them over the trauma, they all had one. I have lost count of the number of spiders I have caught. Never have I received a cream cake for my efforts.

Come to think of it, I haven't had too many rewards for swabbing the decks.

BROUGHT TO BOOK
IF WE BREAK THE RULES

Good heavens, I thought as I browsed through the shelves in the bookshop. My eyes had homed in on a particular volume and suddenly it all became clear. The reason meals arrive at erratic times. Why she is always late when we are going anywhere. Mrs H has been slaving over a hot word processor. She has written a book. "Over 400,000 copies sold" trumpeted the jacket.

It was the title that gave it away. "How to argue and win every time". It had to be by Mrs H. She's an expert. She has a 100% success record in this department. Then I spotted the author's name. It was not written by Mrs H at all but by a man!

I decided not to invest in this tome, especially as it was by a mere male. I defy any man to have the wherewithal to out manoeuvre Mrs H let alone set it down in print. Anyway, the Fortress library is already stocked with a fair number of books.

Many of them are reference books. These are volumes that the word-hungry Mrs H has gathered to assist us along life's highway. There are medical books, gardening and cookery books. Books with household hints. There are even a few DIY books on the shelves. Mrs H has purchased these in a bold but fruitless attempt to instil some practical skills in her useless husband.

In fact, I do wish Mrs H would write a book. My fellow inmates and I could do with some sort of manual. We could hang it by a bit of string in the kitchen to refer to when we are given our jobs. It would be a bit like the Highway Code. Except that not all drivers obey the Highway Code whereas we foot soldiers at Fortress H are expected to stick rigidly to Mrs H's rules. There are just so many to remember.

Open a pack of sealed bacon with a pair of kitchen scissors. Don't use a knife; it blunts the blade. Store the jar of peanut butter upside down in the cupboard or you'll always use the runny mixture at the top and leave an unspreadable lump at the bottom

Actually I am quite well programmed already, as I discovered the other night. I was washing up a chopping board after Mrs H had been preparing some meat. A little voice in my head said: "Make sure and wash this up well. It's had raw meat on it." I scrubbed it hard feeling rather cocky that I had remembered my training. My glory was short lived.

Brat Major was feeling a bit sorry for herself. She had a sore throat and a bit of a cold. I was helping her to make a hot lemon and honey drink. She got out a mug and ladled much more than the permitted amount of honey into it. I squeezed the juice out of the lemon and was about to add it to the honey when Mrs H intervened.

"Stop!" she yelled. I performed an emergency stop, put on my mental handbrake and slipped my brain into neutral. "You shouldn't pour the boiling water onto the lemon," she said in an incredulous voice that made me feel as though I had just extracted two live wires from the mains and was about to touch them together. "If you do that, you'll destroy all the vitamin C. Add the lemon to the water and honey." Now if this had been in Mrs H's reference book, I could have looked it up before I embarked on my chore and avoided all that grief.

I did as I was told, not entirely convinced that plunging the lemon into the hot water was any different to doing it the other way round. Satisfied that we were now operating within the correct guidelines Mrs H headed out of the room. As she reached the door she swung round. Her eyebrows strained to meet as she frowned in my direction.

"And I hope you washed that chopping board up well. I've had raw meat on it." I donned my best self-righteous look and was radiating smugness but it was all to no avail. She was gone. Having delivered her statement she had headed off to wield her machete at other dense areas in the Fortress jungle of domestic strife.

I find the toughest thing about being pre-programmed is when we are at other peoples' houses. It is hard to remember that the Fortress rules do not necessarily apply. I've had to restrain myself from diving to slip a coaster under somebody's cup of coffee before it hits the table. And the times I've wanted to unplug the television when we get up to go home!

Perhaps there is an opportunity here for Mrs H to market her book. I wonder if she'd let me write a chapter on washing up.

CHEESED OFF WITH MRS H'S FROMAGE-FREE SOUFFLÉ

I fear that Mrs H's mind continues to deteriorate. She's going through a particularly bad patch at the moment. It started last Thursday in the supermarket. She was about to hurl some chilled ravioli into her trolley when she realised her coat and handbag were in the way. The trouble was, she hadn't taken a coat. And her handbag was over her shoulder. She had hijacked somebody else's trolley. She was forced into an embarrassing search of the aisles for the rightful owner.

Then we had the incident of the cheese soufflé. I arrived home from work to be informed that all at once she desperately fancied a cheese soufflé. Oh no, I thought, sudden cravings? Not pregnant, please!

Eagerly she prepared her soufflé and popped it into the oven. First problem; the bulb that lights the oven had gone. Panic!

"I won't be able to see if it's rising," she wailed. "And I can't open the oven door 'cos it'll spoil it!" I fetched a torch and we were treated to the bizarre spectacle of Mrs H shining the light through the oven door, hooting with excitement as she watched her effort cook to perfection.

"Look at that," she exclaimed in delight. Then she hooted again - but this time it wasn't with excitement.

"Oh no!," she exploded. "I've left the cheese out." I ask you, whoever heard of a cheese soufflé without the cheese? But sure enough, three ounces of freshly grated cheese was grinning at us from the worktop. Undaunted, we plonked everything on to our plates and sat down to what you might call an MFI soufflé. Self-assembly.

I put a new bulb in the oven the following day. This is quite a speedy turn round compared with the number of items at Fortress Haverson awaiting replacement. Unfortunately none of them are within the budget so we make do and improvise. We have lived with some of these faulty things for quite a while. It brings to mind that most apt of phrases, familiarity breeds acceptance.

Take the freezer for example. Years ago the hinges on the lid gave up the ghost. This meant we had to hold the lid up with one hand while extracting food with the other. That may not sound too bothersome until you are faced with the challenge of having a good one-handed rummage.

You just try it. Put one arm behind your back and see if you can heave a frozen chicken out when it is buried deep under a loaded basket.

We took to wedging the lid open with a plastic container. Eventually we got round to doing something about it. A man arrived with a set of hinges, took one look and announced that we needed a new lid. A few days later he returned only to discover that our freezer was so old that he was faced with attempting to fit a metric lid to an imperial hole. There was nothing he could do.

The freezer was in perfect working order so we have spent the last few years quite happily wedging the lid open. Our children have been brought up with it. They probably think all chest freezers come complete with a piece of Tupperware.

It gets worse. We have a ring on the electric cooker which formed a splinter group from the other three. If we leave the cooker on at the mains, this rogue ring switches itself on and off at will. Therefore, for the last few years the cooker has had to be turned off at the mains after use.

The times one of us has put a saucepan on the stove only to find a couple of minutes later there is no activity whatsoever because we have forgotten to switch it on at the socket.

We did persuade a man to come and look at it once. He scratched his chin and thought yes, he could probably fix it. He left to order some parts. That was three years ago. We haven't seen him since.

Now the video has begun to disintegrate. The eject button decided it had had enough and retreated somewhere inside the machine. But the inner knob to which it was once attached was accessible through the vacated rectangular gap. All we needed was something the right shape to push through this slit.

A bit of Haverson improvisation came to the rescue and after only a couple of weeks we have all got quite used to the revised method of ejecting videos. And no one has asked why we always have a toothbrush beside the video recorder.

I can't help wondering if Mrs H has adopted the "familiarity breeds acceptance" philosophy with me. She's probably got so used to me by now that she thinks all husbands spend their lives striving to please their wives in the continuing pull towards the common good. Of course they don't!

Do they?

MRS H REALLY TAKES MY BREATH AWAY

Summer is rattling away at an alarming rate. Already the three Haversons who either attend or are employed at local schools have been on holiday for a week. Two are bored and irritable, one is frazzled. I'll leave you to work out which is which.

End of term brought all the usual school activities plus a few more. The school play was a cracker. A first-class performance took a light-hearted look at the voyages of Captain Cook. It was all the more entertaining on the first night when the troupe inadvertently shuffled the scenes.

They jumped from scene 6 to scene 8 and then headed back to scene 7 - I think! The good captain took his crew to the Antarctic then wound up buying furs from the Indians to keep the shipmates warm when they sailed to where they had just been - if you see what I mean.

The cast were magnificent. With the help of a few ad libs they carried on in the true tradition of the theatre and earned deserved warm applause from their appreciative audience.

Then there was the PTA barbecue. Bags of booze and burgers together with the best incentive I can think of not to sustain an injury. Remember GBH who used to be our neighbour and works with Mrs H at the school? The one who can reduce me to a gibbering wreck by just looming into view? Well, she was in charge of the first aid. The prospect of her being let loose on me with a bandage and a safety pin was enough to make me tread very, very carefully.

The term finally concluded with the school staff's soiree. We gave GBH a lift to it. I seem to remember offering transport to her at the barbecue after I'd sunk a couple of sherbets. Or maybe it was the threat of a dab or two with iodine that caused me to be so generous.

GBH is as bad as Mrs H in many respects. She phoned twice while we were getting ready for the "do" to put back the departure time as she was running late. Of course, this was fine by Mrs H who was well behind schedule herself. It didn't matter how many circuits of the hall I paced jangling my car keys, for once she wasn't totally to blame.

The journey was a distance of around four miles. As soon as the two of them were together in the car it was as though someone had thrown a switch. They went into full yak.

There was a brief pause at one stage. They weren't stuck for conversation. It was just their perpetually active brains sifting through the gossip to sort out which juicy bit was next for the mangle.

The silence almost prompted me to speak. Instead I waited to see how long they could sustain the hush. It lasted for one tenth of a mile. Pretty impressive bearing in mind they hadn't seen each other for almost four hours.

Now, there must be a collective name for teachers. A chalk of teachers? Or maybe a curriculum of teachers. How about an assembly of teachers? Anyway, there we all sat taking advantage of the balmy summer evening, enjoying a fine spread. Conversation was varied. Among the riveting topics was the one put forward by Brat Minor's teacher. "Do you know," he announced. " I bleached my patio last weekend?" Perhaps that explains a few things about the youngest Haverson.

But in spite of the convivial company this evening was, as were all the other events I have mentioned, tinged with sadness. It had been the head teacher's last term. He is taking a teaching post abroad and this was the last time we would all be together.

He will be missed. But not just for the considerable good work he has done for the school. I have lost an ally. This man, who bravely took Mrs H into his employ, had, over the last few months, begun to emerge from the closet and support my case as the Fortress H underdog.

Earlier this year I was able to quote in this column his admission that he was coming round to my way of thinking where Mrs H is concerned. Now we have something in writing from him supporting this. To mark his departure the outgoing Mortarboard presented each member of staff with a certificate which was awarded for a particular "quality" he had spotted during their career. Mrs H's was for " The Longest Breath".

Spot on! When she talks she has the ability to squeeze optimum mileage out of a single intake of oxygen. There are no pauses. The listener has no opportunity to interrupt. Indeed, I find myself breathing for her when she is in full flow.

I would tell you what GBH got her certificate for. But I'm still having nightmares which feature the indiscriminate use of iodine.

WHEN FORTRESS H GOES ON HOLIDAY

There should be a place where you can board young humans for the duration of a holiday. You leave your pampered feline at a Cattery so why not an equivalent for children? A Brattery perhaps.

Drop the dears off the night before you depart. Leave their favourite toys, a blanket and a few instructions. "She likes a Mars Bar just before she goes to bed. Oh and if his hair needs washing you'll have to make him do it. But be careful, he hates it so much he goes wild and scratches."

I am moved to suggest this after a couple of weeks on holiday in the company of two children who protested at practically everything Mrs H and I wanted to do. We did our best to interest them but in return they whinged at walking, moaned about monuments and cursed at castles. Then, when it was all over, they told everyone what a great time they had! Especially the place where we stayed.

In fact it was all a bit surreal, like the plot of the late-night movie. You know the ones where the innocent family arrives in a picturesque village and everything looks perfectly normal. But things are not all they seem.

This year, Herefordshire was the target for the annual relocation of Fortress H chaos. We stayed in a lovely old house, well off the beaten track. But no sooner had we arrived than odd things began to happen.

Bits of furniture fell apart. We opened the fridge and the door to the freezer compartment just dropped off. Doorknobs inexplicably came away in our hands. Some postcards vanished into thin air.

And the loo door had hinges which added to the atmosphere. They must have been a relic from a Hammer Horror film set. Every time the door creaked open I expected Vincent Price to emerge. The bed that Mrs H and I had also made eerie noises. It groaned like a galleon nosing its way through a moderate swell.

One night I thought it was pelting with rain but when I peered outside, armies of giant moths were attacking the window. We were awoken on our first morning by what sounded like gun shots. We reassured ourselves that it was only a bird scarer. But if it was, how come we never heard it again? Did the local winged population get the message at the first bang or was there something more sinister?

The lady who owned the house was a real character. She greeted us with such a volley of chatter I thought Mrs H had finally met her match in the talking department.

But what a professional Mrs H is. She rallied and her jaws were soon operating like a well oiled machine. After a few minutes they were babbling excited irrelevancies at each other as only women can. But our delightful landlady served only to fuel our spooky feelings about the strange goings on.

"Be wary of the local pub," she warned. "Some people had a meal there and the landlord's dog nicked a sausage off one of the plates. They complained and he said, 'Don't worry dear. I won't charge you for it.'"

"And don't go in the village shop," she advised. "You'll come out with all sorts of things you didn't want." She went on to describe a shop on a par with Arkwright's in Ronnie Barker's Open All Hours. "Someone went in for a paper and came out clutching three bread rolls. And one of my guests went in to get something for a sore throat. They got a packet of Tunes; three years past its sell-by date! They took them back and were told, 'This is a village shop, not a supermarket'."

Of course, all this made it one place we simply had to visit. After a week we summoned the courage to cross the threshold. They must have wondered what was going on when the entire Haverson family filed into the tiny shop under the pretext of buying a pint of milk.

"Do you want a daily paper?" barked the lady behind the counter as I discretely checked the sell-by date on the milk.

"Yes please," I replied, thinking I was getting off lightly.

"Well we've run out," she replied bluntly. "I'll save you one for the rest of the week."

"No...it's...er ...all right. Thanks," I stammered and with that we fled, falling over each other in our efforts to get out the door.

Then there were the sheep. I looked out of the window one afternoon and literally hundreds of sheep were stampeding down the lane. Do Herefordshire sheep migrate in mid-August or was this part of some bizarre ritual? They disappeared over the brow of the hill and were never seen again. Where had they come from?

We tracked the droppings along the road. They suddenly appeared on the tarmac in the middle of nowhere. No field gate or farmyard in sight. Mind you, it wasn't too far from a certain village shop.

CRY? NOT ME,
I'M BATTLE-HARDENED

I read a survey in the EDP on what makes us cry and came to the conclusion that I have more fortitude than I thought. For example, over 21% of men cry when they receive criticism. As I am consistent in my inability to achieve the rigorous standards set by Mrs H, criticism is not unfamiliar to me. But not once has she reduced me to tears.

Similarly, in spite of the healthy set of lungs Mrs H possesses, I have not joined the near 10% of males that have a good howl when someone yells at them. I am particularly proud of this because not only can Mrs H make the windows rattle when she lets fly but also she often throws in the element of surprise.

I demonstrated my resilience only the other day. I was alone, immersed in my own thoughts. Suddenly Mrs H entered dramatically stage right clutching a tube of toothpaste. She was actually airborne as she kick started the vocal chords.

"Is anybody ever going to finish this toothpaste?" she bawled so that those not in the room could also share the message. Now, it was 11 o'clock in the morning, not the peak time for brushing the molars. Mrs H had produced a secret weapon; she had added confusion to her armoury.

The problem is this. When we get almost to the end of the toothpaste, it is a chore to extract the last half-inch so someone will start a new tube. We all transfer to it and the old one gets abandoned. This irks the thrifty Mrs H. She can't finish the job herself. She uses special toothpaste because she has sensitive teeth. No doubt due to all the gnashing they do.

Then last week I thought I'd pushed Mrs H into the 71% of women who cry when their feelings are hurt. As soon as I opened my mouth I knew she'd take the hump. "Had a smashing meal in the canteen today," I announced. I should have stopped there because, as I went on to describe the Hawaiian chicken served on a bed of rice accompanied by baby sweet corn, I could see the heckles begin to rise.

"Well, perhaps you better eat there more often then," she rejoined huffily. Having got this far I became blasé with bravado and dug myself in deeper.

"Perhaps I should. When I asked what was on offer I was given a choice of six dishes. No one said, 'Oh I haven't decided what to cook yet'. I didn't have to amuse myself for over two hours before it was ready. And I wasn't sent out to get the washing in while I waited."

At this point I felt I'd pushed my luck far enough. Whilst the survey says that two thirds of women cry when someone close is injured, it doesn't indicate if that applies when they are the ones responsible for inflicting the pain.

A third of women cry when a valued possession is lost. Mrs H almost entered this category when her beloved combination microwave broke down. It has been taken away for repair and its loss has struck at the very heart of Fortress catering. The way she carried on you'd think there are no other means of cooking a meal. They didn't have microwaves when man lived in caves and they managed to heat the leftovers from the previous day's wild hog pot roast.

The machine stopped suddenly in the middle of baking a cake. This is tantamount to anarchy at Fortress Haverson. It's the equivalent of me abandoning ship in the middle of the washing up.

What made matters worse was that nobody noticed the wretched thing had ground to a halt. The truculent teenager was the last person seen in the general vicinity so she got the blame. But when it happened three more times and she was nowhere in sight, we realised something was wrong.

Without it Mrs H's routines are in disarray. We are presented with frozen bread because she doesn't remember to get it out in time to defrost. She forgets that, unlike the microwave, the cooker doesn't switch itself off when the timer goes so we had pulped apple pie for Sunday lunch.

After a week she learnt that, owing to holidays, the repairers hadn't even looked at it. I thought she was going to burst a blood vessel. "I don't know how I am managing without it," she exploded. "Everyone should have one you know. They save electricity and make life so much easier."

All this over an inanimate object. What would happen, I wonder, if I was taken away for a couple of weeks? Would she get as upset? Even burst into tears? After all, 41% of women cry when they're missing a loved one.

Mind you, 33% of them cry when they're happy. In Mrs H's case, exactly which emotion triggered the weeping could be open to debate.

UNDER THE SPELL
OF MYSTIC MOG

I think I've just set the endurance record for any of my struggles at Fortress Haverson. Five years is a long time to stave off the inevitable but with odds of three to one against I suppose I was bound to cave in eventually.

Over two years ago I told in this column of the continuing pressure I was under to get another cat. "Fortress Haverson will remain petless," I wrote. Alas the writer has eaten those bold words. I have conceded defeat and now occupy fifth place in the Fortress pecking order. Mystic Mog has joined the payroll. He is nine lively inches of inquisitive black fur.

Throughout those five years I based my arguments for maintaining a feline-free environment on memories of all the hassles that came with our previous four-legged incumbents. They possessed voracious appetites and were allowed to flout every Fortress rule.

I recalled such horrors as cleaning out cat litter having just Hoovered one of Mrs H's Aubergine Bakes. Disposing of the deceased hunting trophies which were left on the doorstep. Or worse, dealing with the ones that were still kicking. Getting up in the night when the intrepid hunters returned in the early hours and demand access to a slumbering Fortress H with persistent wailing.

As my resolve weakened I embarked on a damage limitation exercise. If we had to have a cat, maybe I could salvage some dignity by having no involvement whatsoever with the day to day maintenance of the animal. To my disappointment this condition was accepted. The children even agreed to scale down their expectations at Christmas and birthdays to help pay the Whiskas bill.

I had been outmanoeuvred. Mystic Mog has now moved in and taken over our lives. Even transforming the way my fellow inmates talk. They have adopted mogspeak. They communicate with the kitten in a virtually unintelligible language that would arouse disdain in the newest born baby. "Aahh, ooose a dood 'ittwle boy nen?"

After a couple of weeks he made his first serious dent in the chequebook. He went to the vet for his jabs. I came home to find literature on exterminating cat fleas, tablets for roundworm and a bill for over £30.

Then I stumbled across Mrs H studying what I thought was a recipe book. "Hey, this is good!" she exclaimed. Oh good, I thought. She's found something different to do with an Aubergine. Sadly not.

"There's an excellent suggestion in this book on how to get cats to pass hairballs," she babbled excitedly as if she'd just focused her telescope on a hitherto undiscovered planet. You may imagine that my reply contained just the merest hint of sarcasm.

Mystic Mog is programmed with the full repertoire of cute kitten antics. He chases table tennis balls, gets tangled up in bits of string and hides in corners to make random assaults on unsuspecting ankles.

He was fully house trained when we got him. But of course, if you're nine weeks old and busy entertaining humans, you simply can't stop to take time out to go in search of your cat litter.

Mystic Mog solved the problem by dashing into a particular corner of the north wing, doing his business then returning to the arena for more fun. He was puzzled when three of those two-legged creatures that just seconds ago had been falling about laughing at him let fly hysterical screams, disappeared in various directions before returning armed with buckets of water, cloths and disinfectant.

And why did the fourth one remain in the armchair with that smug "I told you so" look on his face?

To remind him of the correct procedure, every so often one of them grabs the bewildered animal and unceremoniously plants him in the cat litter. I wonder how they would like it if they were watching telly and someone suddenly seized them and plonked them on the loo.

Thanks to Mrs H, there is one typical kitten frolic he cannot perform too well. Chasing his tail. When we first had him Mrs H noticed he had a kink at the end of it. She mentioned this to the vet who said it was matted hair and promptly dangled him under the tap to clean it.

A week later the truculent teenager noticed a sore place where this kink had been. Armed with some cotton wool and warm water Mrs H decided to bathe it. Carefully she drew the swab along his tail.

"Oh no!," she screamed. "The end of his tail has come off." She opened the cotton wool and sure enough, there was a little black stump about half an inch long. He had suffered no pain and carried on playing as if nothing had happened. He still chases his tail but now he doesn't always catch it.

My concern was not so much for Mystic Mog. But if Mrs H can do this to a kitten's tail, what could she do to me?

MRS H IS ARMED
AND DANGEROUS

If you're passing Fortress Haverson one autumn evening, you may spot a face at the window. Nose pressed against the glass, eyes peering anxiously into the night sky. It will be me. I'm monitoring the phases of the moon.

As Mrs H continues to push back the frontiers of bizarre behaviour I have decided to see if there is a pattern to her antics. Her peculiar outbursts come in fits and starts so if I can find a common denominator such as a full moon, I can at least plan ahead. Make sure I am out that night or ensure all the doors and windows are secured.

I've grown accustomed to the odd brainstorm. Like the other night when she squeezed a lemon; threw the peel into the washing up bowl and the squeezer in the bin. But it's the sudden irrational surges that worry me. It was after she got involved in the catfight that I decided the time really had come to try and get one step ahead.

It was about half past ten one night. We were watching television. Well, that's not strictly true. I was in front of the box but, as usual, Mrs H was optimising time dealing with an outbreak of ironing.

She can be quite annoying when she tries to concentrate on television and press a shirt. She hears what's going on but if she doesn't happen to glance towards the screen at the right moment she misses an important visual incident. She expects me to keep her up with the plot. "What happened to the man with the bald head?"

"Oh he fell off the multi-storey car park before the last commercial break." I've got so used to this that I've slipped into the habit of providing verbal subtitles. "Did you see that? He slipped a gun under his pillow."

Anyway, there we were, Mrs H listening and me commentating, when the lounge door opened. Brat Major, the truculent teenager, entered. She announced that Brat Minor had alerted her to the sound of two cats revving up for scrap beneath his bedroom window. Would one of us kindly deal with them as the mournful wailing was disturbing their sleep.

"You're supposed to turn a hose on them," said Mrs H with a glint in her eye. All the signs were there that she was boiling up for a funny turn. I decided not to get involved. I had no intention of dragging the hose out of the shed at that time of night so she could have a mad moment under the pretence of stopping a bit of fur flying.

Unfortunately Brat Minor fuelled his mother's mania by offering the loan of his water gun. Actually it's more like a cannon. It comes complete with reserve tank giving it a camel-like capacity which sustains the young man through lengthy pursuits of his sister guaranteeing she'll end up with a good soaking.

How he acquired this weapon almost rivals the Arms to Iraq scandal. He turned up with it one day saying he had borrowed it from a friend. When, weeks later, he was still administering a drenching to anyone that strayed into his exclusion zone, we probed a bit deeper.

He then claimed he had hired it from the friend. Now Brat Minor and money are not easily parted so we pressed him further. Finally he confessed he had bought it off the friend only to discover that he had made, for him, a rare error of financial judgement. Apparently he could have purchased a new one almost as cheap.

Back to the feline fracas. By now, Mrs H had worked up a good head of steam. She seized the gun and was about to go over the top when she realised she hadn't a clue how to fill it let alone shoot the wretched thing. She had to delay her assault while Brat Minor conducted a hasty training session in water weapons.

With a full tank, Mrs H leapt into the night. She circumnavigated Fortress H until she reached the battlefield where two snarling cats were about to engage in paw to paw combat. Issuing a blood-curdling yell, she unleashed a powerful jet of water. Such was their panic, both scarpered in the same direction. I am not sure which scared them most, the water or the sudden appearance of this demented woman.

There has been no talk of this incident around the village so hopefully none of the neighbours witnessed the rampant Mrs H. But one of her other blips could still go public - if Brat Minor loses his footwear.

Mrs H was marking his name in his new shoes. "Oooh!" she giggled. "Look what I've done!" She had written, in indelible ink, her maiden name. Well, we've only been married 23 years.

Maybe I missed a full moon that night. Or was she trying to tell me something?

PLAYING SECOND FIDDLE
TO THE CAT

I have received a serious complaint following last week's column. It concerns the part where I recounted how a swashbuckling Mrs H rampaged round the garden late one night. Armed with Brat Minor's water gun, she sprayed water indiscriminately to break up a catfight. I described this behaviour as somewhat "bizarre".

"What," raged the complainant, "is so strange about that. How else would you break up a cat fight?"

Fortunately I don't see this one getting as far as the Press Complaints Commission. In case you're thinking there must be another one out there like Mrs H, I can reveal that the person who lodged the complaint was none other than the lady herself. She could see nothing unusual in playing her war games in the dark.

"I do hope people don't think I actually sprayed the cats," she said indignantly. "I only squirted it in their general direction. What else was I to do? I would have used a bucket of water but I didn't want to soak them." I thought that was the object of the exercise.

I had forgotten about Mrs H's eccentric behaviour in the feline department until I spotted one of her famous lists. These are the many aide memoirs that she leaves scattered around Fortress H. They help her control the host of activities that either she does or the rest of us are bidden to perform in the pull towards the common good.

To the untrained eye, these lists are heavily coded. My attention was drawn to this particular one because it had my name on it. There were three scrambled prompts. The first: "Neil - stick window sill" I decoded as being a loose tile in Brat Major's bedroom which I had been under pressure to repair for some time.

Then there was the bewildering: "Elephants in paper." After some deep brain searching for a rational explanation I recalled an "Are you listening to me?" conversation we'd had. There had been an article in the newspaper about elephants. Mrs H wanted to keep it and I had been ordered to retrieve it from the old papers in the shed. Another task I had failed to execute.

The last note brought my knees together. "How old when neutered?" Well, I know I've been meaning to stick that tile for quite a while but surely, this was a bit drastic. Then all became clear. A black blur flashed past in hot pursuit of a table tennis ball. It was Mystic Mog, the new four-legged addition to the Fortress payroll. He played around without a care in the world, blissfully unaware that his doting owner was lining him up for the bread knife.

I searched my soul for some sympathy but it was hard work. When he joined the household I said he had nudged me down to fifth in the Fortress pecking order. I believe now, that I have in fact slipped to sixth. Such is the contrast between the attention lavished on Mystic Mog and the sheer neglect of yours truly that I think they have left a spare place in the hierarchy. Just in case something else more important than me comes along.

I arrive home from work to hear the cry go up: "Has anybody fed the little sweetie?" All hands descend on the vast store of cat food and they debate what flavour "the dear little chap" would like.

The Truculent Teenager lies on the floor beside him watching as he devours each mouthful. Brat Minor meanwhile provides entertainment for him by leaping around the food bowl with the table tennis ball. Me? Well, I mooch around with a rumbling stomach; safe only in the knowledge that I will get fed eventually. Even Mrs H has to stop to eat.

One night, to kill time, I went to the shed in search of the elephant's article. I had abandoned ideas of ingratiating myself by diving into empty paper bags and curling up lovingly in cardboard boxes. Perhaps if I could find that news item I would be rewarded with food.

My journey to the shed proved painful. Life can be so cruel. From surrounding houses came the aroma of evening meals being prepared. I busied myself by trying to identify which neighbour was having what for tea.

"I think they're having chicken next door," I announced when I returned, minus the elephant's article. This failed to cut any ice with Mrs H.

"Bully for them," she replied without emotion as she organised a working party to clean out the cat litter.

I know what I'll do. I'll invest in a small plastic bowl. I will inscribe it with the word "Neil" and place it beside the one marked "Puss". I can get used to eating from a crouched position. I'll probably get a bit of indigestion but at least I'll get some grub.

I'm not too sure about the menu though. Anybody ever tried chunky beef and liver in nourishing jelly?

START THE DAY
THE FORTRESS WAY

The time is 7.15 am. I am moving smoothly through the early morning routines. My main task is to sound reveille and galvanise the other inmates of Fortress H into action. Any time left over is spent on getting myself ready for work. By the time other sleepy heads are staggering around I am performing my allotted dawn duties with robotic efficiency.

Pour muesli in bowl, quick mouthful before setting hot water tap running. Fill washing up bowl, another mouthful of muesli and add washing up liquid - to washing up water not muesli. Gulp of orange juice, yell at Brat Minor to get up and plead with Brat Major to help with lunch boxes.

Stuff mouth full of muesli to enable sustained munching during washing up. Dry hands, more museli, more orange juice. Yell at Brat Minor again; grab tea towel, more muesli, dry first intake of breakfast things.

"Have you told him to get up yet?" shouts Mrs H from the bathroom.

Yell at Brat Minor; grab remainder of museli, trip over Mystic Mog. Clean muesli off floor, yell at Mystic Mog, yell at Brat Minor, yell at Brat Major. Think about yelling at Mrs H but common sense comes to the rescue. Change for work. They're on their own now.

It was at this point the other day that an otherwise normal morning took a slight deviation. As I pulled on my shirt, I discovered a button missing. So well honed are the early morning timings that it only takes something like this to throw my entire routine out of sync.

By the time I had found a fresh shirt with its full compliment of buttons, I was running late and ended up dashing for the car. It would have been of no great importance but this was the second time in a matter of days this had happened. The first shirt with the AWOL button was still in the Fortress sewing department. Experience tells me it could be there for some time.

Later that same day I had to see one of the senior bosses, one who can influence the Haverson career. As I sat down in his office I felt this gentle breeze blow round my midriff. Can you believe it? Another button had popped along the way.

I spent the entire meeting sitting bolt upright holding my tie firmly over the exposed chunk of escaping stomach.

When I arrived home I complained bitterly to Mrs H that her management of the Fortress Sewing Department left something to be desired. Now before you have a go at me, yes, I can sew a button on. But when I offer, Mrs H goes all self-righteous and says it's not my job. I should be doing other things around the house.

On the surface this sounds as though she is playing the part of the good little woman. In fact it is her back door way of having a dig at me about all the bits of home maintenance I have on my "To do" list.

Mind you, buttons are not the only thing which Mrs H has on her "To do" list. I took the opportunity to whinge that the loop on my raincoat has been awaiting repair for some weeks.

"Well you must remind me," admonished Mrs H. Surely the fact that it lies under the peg in the hall more than it hangs on it is a fair hint that some action is overdue. I pointed out also that she gets extremely testy when I have the temerity to labour a point.

"You have to remind me tactfully," she explained. What! That's like asking someone to light the blue touch paper but without the use of a match. This all ended up with Mrs H delivering her "I don't know where the time goes" speech. This was followed by an equally vehement assertion "How do other people manage to fit everything in?"

I have often wondered this too. Then I had an idea. We have students at the office who come on work experience placements. That's what Mrs H needs, a stint in another household to pick up a few tips.

So is there anybody out there willing to offer Mrs H a work placement? Have her stay for a week to learn how you fit in all the little jobs like sewing and getting your husband's tea before the watershed. Demonstrate how to communicate with children in a voice that doesn't register on the Richter scale.

While we're on the subject of the children, could you take the younger Haversons too? Teach them how to turn taps off; close doors without rattling the foundations of the house. Show them that not every child in the Northern Hemisphere has a guinea pig, a rabbit and a gerbil. And gets most of their father's salary as pocket money.

But hang on a minute. If they were all missing, who would look after Mystic Mog and me?

BRIEF ENCOUNTER
WITH AN OLD FLAME

I have been seeing another woman. Actually she's an old flame. She lived with me some years ago. We spent the best part of last week together. She moved in on the Monday and I hope she'll decide to stay.

We spent time just talking. Breakfast was a sociable affair, not the stressful exercise I am used to. She even helped me with the washing up.

We went out for a meal and I showed her off to friends. Ironing? Yes she pressed my shirts. But ironing all night? Not this lady. She sat next to me on the sofa with a glass of wine while we watched a film.

I know what you're thinking, depending which camp you're in. Either you're saying: "How dare he two time a fine woman like Mrs H!" Or you're nodding knowingly: "About time. Surprised he's stuck it this long."

What did the children think of all this? Did they accept this new woman in their father's life? I doubt they spotted the difference. You see, my new lady is in fact the old one. Well, to be more precise, she's the original model. Let me explain.

Mrs H and I have just spent a week enjoying life as it was. Both children were on school trips at the same time. You can't imagine the feeling of unbridled freedom that surged through us when we were finally alone.

With the Brat hassle removed from the Fortress equation the place took on a new calm and I rediscovered the girl I married. In fact, Mrs H went a whole 24 hours without shouting. Even then it was at the kitten and not me.

Her Truculence was the first to go, dispatched to France early on the Sunday. By order, it was an unemotional farewell. She was mortified when she learned that the most embarrassing thing in her life, her family, was going to be there to see her off. She pleaded for me and her brother to remain in the car while her mother put her on the coach.

In the end we compromised; promising to observe her request for no hugging and kissing. She did mellow as the coach pulled out. A face appeared at the misted window, smiled briefly and graced us with a wave.

Mrs H then went into a series of worry spasms, convinced she had not packed something vital. This was fuelled when the phone rang a mere couple of hours later. But it was a false alarm. It was Her Truculence informing us they had stopped at a service area. For some reason she wanted us to know she was consuming a bag of chips.

Brat Minor made good his escape on Monday morning to nearby How Hill. Again it was a macho departure with his mother being restricted to a perfunctory wave.

I arrived home from work that evening to a silent Fortress H. I passed the window of the north wing. The familiar flicker of the television was absent. Tentatively I put my key in the back door. Now I've always believed this simple act completes a circuit which triggers those indoors to shout at each other.

Usually, as I open the door, there's Mrs H bellowing at the children and them yelling at each other. I get sucked into to it all. Each turns on me to put their case as if I am some kind of arbiter.

"She won't do her homework and he refuses to get changed," moans Mrs H.

"She won't let me play with the kitten," wails Brat Minor.

"He can't have the kitten. He's still got his school clothes on," taunts his sister. They're both clutching a chunk of Mystic Mog and pulling him like a wishbone.

The week sped by. Then a phone call from the truculent teenager reminded us we were still parents. She rang to say she would be home in two hours. "Are you in a good mood Dad?" she slipped into the conversation. Uh oh, here comes the bad news. "I've lost my new sweatshirt," she confessed. Well, I suppose it could have been worse.

Amazingly her brother returned with all his worldly goods intact. But Her Truculence did bring us a small gift each whereas Brat Minor overlooked this gesture. Thoughts of those back home failed to reach his purse.

So the family was reunited. The children were tired and we were nicely relaxed. We drifted into Saturday with hardly a cross word. Then the familiar voice of a roused Mrs H thundered round the house

"Watch your attitude young lady or you'll be in deep trouble!" The spell was broken. My brief reign at number three in the Fortress pecking order, second only to Mystic Mog, was over. I am back to living on my wits.

And what happened to the girl I married? Well, she pops in occasionally. Mind you, the ironing's up to date now.

PEACE FROM MRS H
IS MUSIC TO MY EARS

It is a rare treat for me simply to sit and listen to music. Sadly the pace of life at Fortress Haverson creates few windows for a chap to just flop down and wallow for the entire duration of a CD.

Actually, I think the guilt factor plays a major role in all this. There is always something that needs doing. Mrs H is forever on the go so I too feel obliged to graft away. Becoming immersed in music means all functions can be stood down except the sense of hearing. This inactivity is what makes me feel so guilty.

When I am doing virtually nothing, I feel like a child sneaking its hand into the biscuit barrel, suddenly hearing the sound of heavy footsteps and being caught in the act.

If Mrs H has music on, it serves to inspire her into reaching yet greater heights with her many challenges. We have the Rolling Stones for dusting, a touch of Blues for cooking and Tina Turner weighs in for general duties. You see, Mrs H never does fewer than two things at once. Even if we are out and stop for a coffee, she will produce paper and pen from her bag and start compiling one of her lists.

When I do decide to put on some music, more often than not, the younger generation have commandeered the hi fi and are subjecting it to a dose of speaker-rattling throbbing. Mind you, they don't hang around if I get there first. My music is condemned as "square".

Now there's a good old word from my formative era which is enjoying a Second Coming. As indeed is much of the music that the younger inmates rave about. Many of their favourites are, what I consider, poor remakes of some of the oldies.

In a rare moment of humanity the truculent teenager did pander to my square tastes. She bought me a CD by Michael Crawford. This multi-talented actor has a wonderful voice. Her Truculence presented me with the CD but has made a point of never being in the room when I play it.

Last weekend I broke all the rules. I grabbed a can of beer, crept into the north wing, donned the headphones and settled down for a musical siesta.

My head was filled with beautiful music. I siphoned a couple of mouthfuls of beer. My eyes made representations that they wanted to close. I offered no resistance. I opened them occasionally to execute a successful docking with my beer and to confirm I hadn't gone to heaven.

During one orientation check I was jerked back to reality. It must have been the vibrations. Mrs H was thundering across the room in my direction. I now know what it must be like to lie in the middle of the M25 with a juggernaut bearing down on you.

Usually Mrs H's impending arrival is signalled well in advance. She shouts my name from where ever she is in Fortress H to pinpoint my exact location. Then, to optimise time, she heads towards my voice issuing instructions as she travels. The idea is that by the time she has found me I should be fully briefed. All that remains is for me to clarify any orders that I don't understand.

On this occasion she gesticulated at me to remove the headphones. I made available one ear to receive sound from the outside world; Michael continued to serenade the other. Mellowed by the ale, I was summoning up the courage to issue a refusal to move.

Mrs H pressed her face close to mine. Treating me as if I was hard of hearing she bawled her message. To my astonishment, I was not required to offer any input to driving Fortress life forward.

"Where is your hockey kit? I want to wash it," she yelled. I babbled a response then hastily closed off the ear before any further instructions could be delivered. I watched the departing back of Mrs H; amazed I had been allowed to remain in the armchair.

No doubt she will remind me of this major concession next time I rebel against doing a chore. She will reel off all she achieved while I was allowed to relax.

The arrival of Mystic Mog, the newly recruited Fortress mouse catcher, has brought about a problem should Mrs H and I ever be alone in the house. When I pick up a vocal transmission, I am programmed to await further instructions.

If she fails to manifest herself in front of me I go in search of her. After all, she could be trapped in the tumble dryer. But invariably she can be found clutching the kitten to her bosom and what I heard was her burbling to him in Mogspeak.

"Did you want me?" I enquire.

"Since when," she replies, "Is it you I have grabbed, given a great big cuddle and told you're a little sweetie?"

In my dreams.

MOVING STORY OF
A TRUE ROMANCE

What is it they say? Take a look at her mother because that's what your wife will end up like? I have the evidence. Among our photographs there is one we stumble across occasionally which demands a second look to confirm whether it is of Mrs H or her mum.

There are other clues as to how your future bride will turn out but these don't surface until it's too late. Suddenly you realise she only cooked your favourite meal when she was your girlfriend to please you, her new man. Before you know it you've paid the licence fee, the ring is on your finger - metaphorically it's through your nose - and there are regular servings of the Aubergine Bake.

One of the early signals I missed came to mind the other day when Mrs H and I were in nostalgic mood. We were reminiscing how long we had been living at the current Fortress Haverson. All of a sudden we had donned the rose tinted spectacles and were drifting down memory lane.

Our first house, a good solid dwelling from the era when they built 'em to last. Mind you, with everything in soft focus, we glossed over the fact that I spent an eternity cleaning flaking whitewash off the ceilings before applying emulsion. And all the woodwork was coated in a depressing brown varnish that put up quite a fight when I tried to paint over it.

But the big hint of the Mrs H to be, came well before all that. In fact we weren't even going out together. I was acquainted with what I remember as a rather attractive girl with long dark hair. I bumped into her one day and in the course of conversation she told me she had to move out of her flat and would be staying with a friend until she could find somewhere else.

I believe now that what happened next changed the course of my life. If I hadn't been so chivalrous our relationship may well not have developed and I could now be married to a quiet, compliant adoring woman. Or rich and single without a grey hair in sight.

"I'm moving tonight," she said. "I'm going to hire a taxi to take all my stuff." Yes you've guessed it. Yours truly galloped to the rescue on his white charger. Well, actually it was a Mini.

"Don't do that," I said gallantly. "I'm not busy tonight. I'll move your things in my car."

Mrs H has told me since that she thought, as the Americans say, I was coming on to her. But she was desperate for the help and it was any port in a storm. If she had but known, it never entered my naive head that this could be interpreted as a pass. Had it done, I would have been too terrified to say anything.

I turned up at the appointed time and learnt what was to become a lasting lesson. Mrs H doesn't travel light. Minis are not designed to move such young ladies and their belongings. Nevertheless, I shoved the suitcase in the boot. A host of knickknacks and other personal bits and pieces were piled on the back seat. These were crowned by dresses and the like which came with the instruction "Do not crease".

And there was this small bookcase. It had two shelves and for ease of transport the books were left in it. Boy, was it heavy! Somehow I got it in the car and we made our way to Miss H's temporary gaff.

I was directed to some flats. I parked outside the entrance and leapt enthusiastically out of the car. I heaved the bookcase to the entrance of the flats. "Which one is it?" I asked, eager to get on with the job. By a stroke of luck the flats were opposite a pub which was a regular haunt of mine. Already I could taste the first pint.

"It's that one," she said. I followed the direction of her finger. She was indicating a window on the third storey! To this day, I know not how I got that bookcase up three flights of steps without being condemned to a life trussed up in a surgical appliance.

I should've seen the writing on the wall. This was a forerunner to the "Could you just do" jobs. Here was a woman who could extract my maximum potential.

Worse still, from the window of the flat where she was staying she could see into that pub. So she's had my boozing under scrutiny for over a quarter of a century.

And the bookcase? We've still got it. We had it in a downstairs room we set aside for the children. One day Mrs H said "That would be ideal in Brat Minor's room. Could you just take it upstairs?"

I'm not as young as I used to be. This time I took the books out first.

BLACK HOLE HAS
A MIND OF ITS OWN

There is one cranny of Fortress Haverson which I do my best to avoid, even more than Brat Minor's squat. Yes I'd rather negotiate his bedroom and risk tripping over the contents of his abandoned school bag or skate across the floor courtesy of a pile of old football magazines than venture into the cupboard under the stairs.

It's one of those tiny boltholes that are dumping grounds for anything that needs shoving out of sight. The vacuum cleaner lives there along with such things as loo rolls, bleach and light bulbs. On one side there are shelves stacked with a multitude of bits and pieces while on the other the wall is festooned with anything that will hang. On the back of the door is a carrier bag stuffed full of other carrier bags. Once inside you are surrounded.

Cat swinging is not recommended. Just to get in and out of the cupboard you have to possess the skills of Houdini. And if you want to get right to the end where the stairs meet the ground some knowledge of potholing is essential. It is impossible to enter the cupboard and withdraw without knocking at least half a dozen things off the shelves or from their hooks.

The other day I burrowed my way in for a screwdriver. As I shoehorned myself through the door, the vacuum hose leapt off its specially designed bracket. I bent to pick it up and the shoe polish plonked itself at my feet. I made to retrieve that and some spare batteries were sent scurrying in all directions.

As I straightened up the carrier bag on the back of the door thumped me on the back of the head before leaping eagerly off the hook and depositing its contents all over the kitchen towels.

I always make my feelings known when I go in there so the minute Mrs H heard the clattering she knew what was coming.

"I hate this cupboard! I'm not picking this lot up. If they're so keen to get to the floor they can stay there." With that I reversed dramatically out to be met by a sniggering Mrs H. Her grin didn't last long. I have to be put in my place even if the things in the cupboard refuse to stay in theirs.

"Well that's fine. So you're going to leave all that lot for me to clear up." I ignored this and strutted bravely away. But deep down I'm a coward and, as usual, when she'd gone I snuk back and picked everything up.

Then one day the worm turned. I was in the kitchen when I heard the stifled rantings of a Mrs H approaching meltdown. She was in the dreaded cupboard and clearly the contents was having the sport with her that normally it reserves for me.

I always get a feeling of well being when Mrs H is in a mood and I am not the object of her disquiet. However, I was soon invited to share this moment with her. She stumbled into the outside world and announced that a packet of "your razor blades have fallen on the floor yet again. And I'm not picking them up!"

"Coo!" I chortled. "You wouldn't let me get away with that."

"I don't care," she wailed. "I've had enough." With that she slammed the cupboard door. This was followed by a couple of lumps from within as something else defected from its shelf. This drove Mrs H to even greater heights of frustration. The power of speech deserted her and she could muster only a series of high-pitched howls.

We are now locked in a battle of wills. Pretty pointless really because we all know there's only one winner when Mrs H and I have a head to head. I'm holding out quite well so far. The razor blades are still on the floor; neither of us will pick them up. I've even bought some new ones rather than touch the ones scattered around the cupboard.

Oh I loath that cupboard! The times I've wriggled in there and cracked my head on the underside of the stairs. And it's bad enough being in there when you can see let alone in the dark but regularly I've plunged myself into pitch blackness by head butting the light bulb which some genius strategically positioned at the very point where it is necessary to bow your head.

Probably my biggest enemy in the cupboard is the folding ironing board. It takes no bidding at all to prove its joints are all in perfect working order. At the slightest nudge it will collapse and snare me in a vice-like grip.

Honestly what chance do I stand? An ironing board like a gin-trap on the inside and Mrs H lurking on the outside.

DRIVEN CRACKERS
AT THE OFFICE DO

It was all rather exhausting. It wasn't just Christmas itself but the whole jamboree. The pre-Yuletide circuit of functions and carol services wears you out after a while. But this year there were some memorable moments.

Take the office do. On the Monday following the bash, a colleague came up to me and said: "At last! I've seen Mrs H in action." He had observed Mrs H bark a command at me and, apparently, my obedience was most impressive.

It all started after the meal. Suddenly, Mrs H set about disembowelling the remains of the Christmas crackers. She explained to puzzled diners that she wanted the cardboard tubes for the school. They were ideal for craftwork. Blue Peter aficionados will know, toilet roll inners are now considered a health hazard.

This prompted a willing response from those around us and soon ten or more tubes had been rescued. It was time then to move to the dance floor so something had to be done with the tubes. Mrs H immediately took control.

"Pick those up," she rasped at me. My colleague tells me that, like a faithful Labrador eager to please, I gathered up as many tubes as I could carry and under close direction from Mrs H hastened to the cloakroom to stash the spoils.

Probably worst of all is that I was not at all embarrassed. It was all quite normal to me. But what must the others have thought? We've all heard of doggy bags but scavenging the remnants of a pulled cracker?

Then there was the combined schools Carol Service at the village church where children from the schools sing, read and play musical instruments. We arrived minutes before the start and had to sit in some overflow seating at the back. Practically every tot who wasn't performing in the service occupied the rest of this block. It was like sitting in a crèche. We were an island in a swirling sea of small humans.

They scraped around on their chairs, burbled to each other and indulged in the occasional skirmish. Scattered among them was the odd parent battling gamely to maintain order. I was quite proud of our two sitting quietly amidst it all. Until that is Brat Major strove through the din to attract my attention.

"Dad! Dad!" she hissed desperately. "Do you know," she said

jabbing a finger in the direction of her brother, "He finished off all the cake tonight." I persuaded her that perhaps this could be debated when we got home.

Then it was Brat Minor's turn. He tugged urgently at my sleeve before saying in one of those loud whispers that children use to impart a secret but which everybody can hear.

"Will we be home in time to watch The Bill?"

Life being so hectic, I was relieved when I drove home from work one night and realised we had nothing on that evening. Fortress Haverson was unusually silent as I garaged the car. A bonus. Mrs H had taken the children shopping after school and was going to be home late.

I headed for the door to wallow in a frictionless Fortress H. I felt in my pocket for the door key; nothing there. Oh no! I must have left it at home in the morning. I knew they wouldn't be too long but what to do in the meantime?

Having cased the joint and found no means of entry, I opened the garage and climbed back into the car to make the most of the lingering warmth. I did wonder whether the neighbours might think I was going to connect a pipe to the exhaust and end it all. Well, either nobody saw me go in or they decided it would be a blessed release so they let me carry on.

I sat there for a full hour. Predictably when the rest of the family arrived home, they thought it all a huge hoot. But as we walked down the path Mrs H suddenly oozed compassion. "Oh the poor thing!" she exclaimed. My little face lit up. Somebody cared. Then she said: "He must be starving!" It was at this point I realised my plight had been dismissed and the sympathy was directed at Mystic Mog.

Later that week, I managed to avoid helping at the school disco. But I did take my son on one side for a bit of chap's talk. I passed on some of my best chat-up lines. "Dad," he said disdainfully, "I think I can see why you never had many girlfriends." Suitably put in my place, I left the room. As I disappeared into the hall, his sister confided in him: "Yea, and look what he did end up with."

Dutifully I informed her mother of this remark. It's a good job it was the season of goodwill.

PAYING THE PRICE
FOR ALL THAT PLASTIC

In just a few days time an envelope containing joyous news form the credit card company will drop through the Fortress letterbox. The full extent of the festive debt will be revealed

My credit card must be suffering from swipe fatigue. I'm surprised some shops didn't challenge my signature which has become decidedly shaky through scribbling my name so many times over the past couple of months.

Sometimes I think Mrs H believes the term "disposable income" means she must ensure all available money must be spent. She's certainly pretty good at that interpretation of it. Just before Christmas she returned from the supermarket waving a receipt that you could attach to the Andrex puppy.

To be fair, recently some of the Fortress finances have been directed at me. Mrs H has launched a desperate bid to bring my wardrobe into the nineties. For once we traipsed from shop to shop for my benefit. Sales assistants and fellow shoppers alike were treated to Mrs H's critical observations of my attributes.

"No, that jumper doesn't tone in with your greying hair. That jacket would look good - if your legs were a bit longer." We did succeed in making the odd purchase. But once we got the goods home and I modelled them in conjunction with items from my current range, all were returned for a refund.

This was rather disappointing, as I am delighted to report that, after years in the wilderness of clothes buying, I have twice flown solo and returned with garments that gained approval. However, it was this recently-acquired confidence that set me up for probably the most severe put down that Mrs H has delivered in years.

"I do like that jacket," I said with a newfound air of knowing my own mind. But clearly I have a long way to go yet. Mrs H's response was instant and uncompromising.

"Now that really is for a younger person," Ouch! And she said it without a trace of compassion.

Our shortage of funds will see Mrs H introduce stark economies. At least we won't go hungry during this period of austerity. Leading up to Christmas, enough food was either imported or manufactured on the premises to sustain us through a siege until Easter.

The prudent Mrs H will reinforce the culture of eking out

tubes of this and bottles of that until no more can be squeezed from them. The lengths to which we go to optimise washing up liquid irritate me the most.

When the container is almost empty it is stood upside down. This means that as I administer a squirt to the washing up bowl, four times as much as necessary is unleashed into the hot water.

Even when the container is so empty I am reduced to crushing it as if I am trying to asphyxiate someone, we're not finished. Mrs H inserts some water to rinse out the dregs. Now I need four times as much as normal to generate even the merest hint of froth.

Then there will be the recycling. Tell me, is there anyone else out there who recycles freezer bags? Mrs H religiously washes them out. She does them in batches of about twenty and spreads them all over the work surface to dry. The rest of us are organised into testing them for punctures.

If they leak they are stored for non-freezer use. The good ones are put back into the system. This does cause problems if the old label is still on. The classic case was when I plucked from the freezer what I believed to be homemade ice cream only to discover I had thawed out some mushroom sauce.

The only other person I've known to recycle freezer bags was my mother. At least Mrs H doesn't go as far as she did. To dry them, she used to peg them on the linen line.

Once I vowed never to have a credit card but now my wallet abounds with the wretched things. I've got debit cards, bonus cards, advantage cards, points cards, charge cards and of course the EDP's own Big News Card.

Now there's a thought. How about the Fortress Loyalty card? Mrs H could issue me with a card which I would submit on satisfactory completion of the "could you just do" jobs. I would earn points to cash in for treats and special concessions.

Washing up would earn say ten points; double points for a greasy Sunday lunch.

I might even have a go at the ironing to add to my tally. And just think of the fun deciding how to spend them. 50 points secure a late pass at the pub. 100 points entitle me to sit for the duration of an entire football match on TV, including half time!

I might even be able to buy my way out of those income disposal trips round the city. No. She'd make sure I never got enough points for that.

ANOTHER RECIPE
FOR FORTRESS TANTRUMS

You walk into a restaurant with a group of people. One of them picks up the menu looks at it briefly before throwing it on the table. "Not that again!" they bellow. "Well I'm not eating any of it." With that they storm out.

You'd probably be a bit annoyed. The chef would be a little hurt too. Well this kind of scene is typical in the kitchen at Fortress Haverson. A Brat walks in, sniffs the aroma to identify what's on the menu and lets fly a barrage of vitriol. The Brat then serves notice of an immediate fast should nothing to its liking be offered for lunch. Mrs H just throws her arms up in despair.

"I'm fed up with trying to cook for this family. There's absolutely nothing I can do that we all like." With that she gives a run down of what appeals to whose pallet. "I'm not cooking two meals. They'll have to eat it or lump it."

I drew her sting the other Sunday when I was given a free choice of vegetables. Sprouts, however, were mandatory. I rejected carrots with the submission that I had consumed sufficient recently to place my night vision on a par with that of a thermal imager.

"How about peas?" I suggested. Mrs H's reply narrowed my options. Apparently the vegetables had to be aesthetically pleasing on the plate.

"They're green like sprouts," she scoffed. Of course, how silly of me even to suggest them! I couldn't come up with an acceptable alternative from what we had in stock. This prompted an exasperated Mrs H to demonstrate how often she has watched Humphrey Bogart in Casablanca.

"Of all the vegetables in all the world you have to want something I haven't got." she exploded. Before any blood was spilled, we compromised. I agreed to have carrots if she could live with peas and sprouts on the same plate.

It's all a bit of a farce because I always eat what she serves up anyway. It's not fair really. The younger inmates throw a wobbly and get their way. Take Brat Minor when recently, he thought the chicken stir-fry was to be served with noodles and not rice.

"I'm not eating noodles. I am NOT eating noodles," he informed the cook with no hint of appreciation for her efforts slaving over a hot wok. For his stubbornness he was rewarded by having a portion of rice cooked specially.

We believe the younger inmates are responsible for vanishing cutlery. If they don't want to finish the meal their mother has lovingly cooked they sneak to the bin to dispose of it. In their haste to dump it before Mrs H can make them eat it, the odd fork or spoon is jettisoned into the rubbish.

We did discover the whereabouts of a missing knife the other night. At 3 a.m. in the morning to be precise. Brat Minor woke us to announce he had been sick in bed. We thought all this was behind us now they are older. But fortunately all the old skills were still there; clean up, change sheets, administer sympathy and back to sleep.

Mrs H and I swung into action like a well-oiled machine and it was during the sheet changing that the mystery was solved. Mrs H delved into the draw under his bed for some spares and hey presto, there was the missing knife, coated in cake from some midnight feast. I should add this was not the reason for his infirmity. The crumbs were in such a state of decomposition that clearly it had been there for some time.

You'd think we never fed our children the way they raid the Fortress larder. In fact they've turned food pilfering into an art form. The other evening I watched Brat Minor sidle up to the flip top bin in the kitchen. He pushed the lid down to gain entry in the normal way but shoved something behind the lid into the back of the bin. I challenged him and, to my surprise, he readily gave me an explanation.

"I'm putting sweet wrappers in the back of the bin so when mum throws something away she won't see them." Not only was this fiendish but it illustrates the degree to which he respects my authority. He was desperate his mother shouldn't find out how much chocolate he was scoffing but clearly sees me as toothless and was quite happy to reveal his little dodge.

Perhaps it was my sudden challenge that shocked him into honesty. Maybe his reply was a shade too spontaneous. Like the one he gave while playing family trivial pursuit recently. He was asked the question: "Who first fixed it in 1975?" His little face instantly lit up. He knew it. He rose out of his seat and with eyes shining he triumphantly delivered his answer.

"Jim'll!"

MORE MELLOW TIMES AHEAD, SO I'M TOLD!

Mrs H positively crowed with delight: "You think I'm peculiar and different," she cried with triumph. "But there are people doing it all over the country."

She was wallowing in the reaction to my question a couple of weeks ago: "Does anyone else out there recycle freezer bags?" This is her practice of washing out the plastic bags to re-use them. The comments and letters I have received confirm there are lots of you recyclers prepared to emerge from the closet.

Mrs Warminger of Sheringham is one. She wrote to me saying: "I'm even guilty at times of doing, as your mother did, pegging them out on the line."

Mrs Nairn of Narborough does this too but she adds: "However, despite the proclivity of our clan chief, I have NEVER dried out my tea bags." That's interesting. Not the bit about the tea bags, even Mrs H doesn't do that, but it sounds as though Mr Nairn is called "clan chief" to make him think he is the head of the household whereas he has no clout at all.

Finally there was Mr Harris of Forncett End. He wrote on the letters page of the EDP last Saturday that his wife is a recycler and he went on to sympathise with my lot at Fortress H. He dangled a straw at which I desperately clutched.

"I have a Mrs H and they do mellow," he says. "After 43 years I can get away with things I never used to be able to." Thank you Mr Harris. It's nice to know there is a light at the end of the tunnel; even though my particular tunnel is another 20 years long.

I am heartened by all your comments. It is a great comfort as Mrs H continues to drive us along the tunnel. Like Nelson at Trafalgar, she who rules the Fortress roost sends out a signal in similar vein. "Mrs H expects every inmate to do their duty."

I seem to have acquired my duties by some form of default. Take my regular chore, the washing up. The rest of them know I'll do it so they just leave it . And sure enough, I do it. The same seems to apply to the bin bags. How about that? Bags again!

It starts with the bin in the kitchen. When it's full, I'm the one that cracks first and empties it. We all keep stuffing rubbish in, packing down what's already in there to squeeze in that last bit of orange peel or illicit chocolate wrapper. Eventually the swing lid won't swing.

Still nobody empties it, me included. Instead we resort to

lifting off the lid to force bits and pieces in. Then something large like a Cornflakes packet comes up for disposal. Does this prompt a bin emptying? No, it is stockpiled behind the bin and the stuffing continues. Eventually I cave in and eject the straining bin liner.

Mrs H is as bad as the rest of them but at least she provides an early warning when the bin needs emptying. I hear the airbrakes sigh followed by the equine snort and I know she has just grabbed some paper towel to clean the lid. Someone, usually a brat, has tried to discretely scrape the remains of their Aubergine Bake into the bulging bin and plastered it all over the lid.

It doesn't stop there. The dustmen come on Fridays. They always have so you would think someone might have the gumption to make sure there was something waiting for them at the bottom of the drive. But if I didn't put the bags out, we'd end up with our own refuse tip at Fortress H.

It's me that goes out on cold winter nights and struggles to tie the tops of overfull bin bags. And there's always something in there that wants to escape. Usually it's an empty bottle that pierces the bag. Well, it's almost empty. As I stagger with arms full of bags to the top of the drive I experience this damp sensation as the dregs from a bottle of Coke trickle down my leg.

And we seem to have so many bags. As we turned out of the drive one Friday before the bin men had been I demanded of Mrs H: "How come we generate so much more rubbish than anyone else in the street?"

For some reason this stung Mrs H and, as we travelled up the road, she conducted a survey of everyone else's rubbish.

"They've got three bags. They've got four. There's five there! Three...five... four. How many have we got?" Yes of course she was right again.

Do they really mellow Mr Harris? It's all right for you; you've served your sentence. How am I going to survive the next two decades? Surely if I sustain my current level of service I'll get time off for good behaviour.

BEHIND THE MICROWAVE
IN FORTRESS STATUS

It had been a bad day. Slowly I dragged myself down the garden path, looking forward to entering the warm bosom of my family. I paused at the door, put on my best hangdog expression and plunged into what I hoped would be a sea of sympathy. Some hopes!

"Don't say a word! We've had an awful day. Everything's gone wrong." Even for Mrs H this was a hostile greeting. She went on to list a day so riddled with banana skins that my problems paled into insignificance. As she was about to launch into the final crisis of the day Brat Major turned a pleading face in my direction.

"It wasn't my fault," she blurted out defensively. "I only closed the door." She pointed to the corner of the kitchen and my worst fears were confirmed. The microwave had gone wrong again.

It developed a fault last year whereby it turned itself off at will. It took 8 weeks to fix. They couldn't trace the problem so bits were systematically replaced until it was virtually rebuilt.

By the time it was returned Mrs H was at her wits end. Such is her reliance on the wretched thing that she would cheerfully have done without me for 8 weeks rather than her precious microwave.

This time the catch had broken off and the door was jammed shut. The interior light had remained on and picked out in its soulful glow were three sausage rolls that the truculent teenager was defrosting for her tea. We gathered round it as if it was some kind of museum exhibit.

"They'll be crawling if we can't get the door open," moaned Mrs H. "Just think of the smell." I shot out a hand to force the door. I withdrew it equally as quick as Mrs H did her impersonation of a sergeant major.

"DON'T!" she barked. " If you break it the insurance company won't pay."

We switched it off at the mains and it lay in state for a couple of days while we did no more than pass reverently by. Every so often one of us would turn it on to monitor the decomposition of the sausage rolls.

On the Saturday I rang the insurance company to action a repair. Oh dear. Things are never straightforward are they? First they informed me their appointed dealer was now in Yarmouth.

The dealer then delivered the news that the days he calls in our area to collect machines for repairs would be the very days the following week that Fortress H was unmanned.

Mrs H became highly agitated, bleating graphic tales of maggots crawling over entombed sausage rolls. She whinged so much I could stand it no longer. I flung the machine in the car and drove the 20 odd miles to Yarmouth.

I left it in the shop and ran. I didn't want to be there when the engineer opened the door and was savaged by three mutant sausage rolls.

You may recall, when we took Mystic Mog, the apprentice Fortress mouse catcher, on the payroll, I claimed I had been pushed into not fifth but sixth place in the pecking order. Sixth because I believed that a spare slot had been left in case something more important came along. I know now that the microwave is that other thing. In fact proof of the level of my profile was demonstrated recently by a couple of hurtful examples.

I had told Mrs H that I would be late home from work the following Wednesday. Her mind is choc-a-bloc with information and some of her mental files are only accessed as matter of necessity so when Wednesday arrived I thought it best to remind her that it would be 7 o'clock before she had the joy of seeing me again.

There was no "Oh that'll make tea late" or anything remotely to suggest that my extended absence would in anyway impact on Fortress life. Instead there was a quite dismissive response.

"'Spect I'll remember when you don't turn up," was the casual observation. Come to think of it, my arrival home usually serves only as an intrusion into the battle between Mrs H and her offspring over their rights to watch programmes on television peopled almost entirely by actors with Australian accents.

Confirmation of Mrs H's attention to detail where I am concerned came a few days later. We were watching a TV programme involving a missing person. "Tell me," the policeman asked the distraught wife. "What was your husband wearing when he left for work." The lady went on to give a detailed description of her husbands clothing. From the person at the ironing board adjacent to me there came an equine snort.

"Humph! If it was me, I wouldn't have a clue what you had on when you went to work this morning."

Thank you dear. I'm the adult male with glasses. You know, the one with the wallet.

SORRY SEEMS TO BE
THE HARDEST WORD

There is a facet of my personality about which Mrs H and I disagree. Well, OK there may be more than one. The particular bone of contention I have in mind is saying sorry. I think I'm quite good at it but Mrs H begs to differ.

It seems my grasp of this social skill is weak. I use the wrong tone of voice and the wrong words - "All right, all right I'm sorry OK?"

And the timing of my apologies - "it's too late now you should have said it straight away" - serves only to make matters worse. Mrs H has no such problems. She's never in the wrong so the need to apologise doesn't arise.

My reason for raising this is that I have offended Brat Minor and wish to demonstrate just how contrite I can be by issuing a public apology to him.

I wish to apologise unreservedly for the humiliation and embarrassment I caused him at Youth Club a couple of weeks ago. In lieu of damages I have made a substantial donation to his chocolate fund and undertaken to go public with an incident where I too was highly embarrassed.

The facts of the case are as follows. On our way to visit someone in hospital, we were to drop the youngest Haverson off at the youth club. With Mrs H nursing a large pot plant we set off. For the entire journey Brat Minor pleaded to be dropped off at the entrance to the car park and not taken to the door where his macho chums would see him with his Mum, Dad and big sister.

In reply, we did our best to wind him up; threatening big hugs and kisses when he was released from the car. As we approached the hall he got ever more desperate.

"Dad, don't turn in. Dad! Dad stop here. DAD!" I couldn't resist it. We drove right up to the door. As he leapt out of the car and rushed towards his yelling mates, I wound down the window and played my ace.

"I hope you've got your vest on!" I shouted in my best fatherly voice.

"That's not fair," chastised Mrs H. "You'll pay for that later," I might add that both Mrs H and her daughter were cackling with laughter throughout the episode. They contributed to Brat Minor's discomfort and did nothing to restrain my childish behaviour.

I arrived a bit later than usual to collect him, giving his friends a chance to disperse. I avoided the subject when he got into the car but we had travelled only yards when he had a go at me.

"I got teased all night," he said grumpily. "Not just for being dropped off by all my family but with Mum carrying a bunch of flowers." Such was his misery that I felt a pang of guilt and offered the deal.

And so to my embarrassing moment, I was at the hole in the wall to draw out some money to sustain Mrs H's spending power throughout the weekend. I was about to insert my card when a colleague spotted me. He crept up behind me, thrust his head at the cash machine and bawled: "Don't let him have any!" The machine promptly obeyed.

I inserted my card, keyed in my pin number and entered the amount of cash. I stood back while the machine gurgled and burped. Then it bleeped and informed me that my pin number was wrong. A queue built up as I went through the procedure again. But the machine remained resolute.

By now I could here feet shuffling impatiently behind me and the buzz of discontented muttering. With the utmost care I repeated all the steps, sure that my pin number was correct. The machine remained unmoved.

I froze with embarrassment but then the machine flashed a message inviting me to withdraw my card. I hastily pressed the button and made good my escape. The half dozen or so people in the queue must have been convinced I was either overdrawn or operating with a stolen card.

As I stumbled away I took out my wallet to replace the card and spotted the cause of the problem. I had been feeding the machine with the wrong card. I made to head back to the cash point but I was met by six pairs of suspicious eyes. Red faced, I legged it and got Mrs H her money from a machine far removed.

Mrs H rarely uses the hole in the wall. But then, why should she when she has me, a human cash point? She simply rattles out the password - "I must have some money!" - and I produce my wallet. Of course, she gets a bit narked if I have forgotten to draw any out. That's when I flash her a message. "All right, all right I'm sorry OK?"

LIGHT RELIEF AFTER DETERMINED STAND

Mrs H wailed: "I don't give a monkey's about the shade. Just fix the light!" At last I scented victory. For once, through shear grit and determination, I had the upper hand in a battle of wills having finally reached the end of my tether.

I don't believe Mrs H thinks I've got a tether let alone would know when I was approaching the end of it. But with the incident of the landing light I had had enough.

The light is positioned outside the airing cupboard. The shade is rather large so when the airing cupboard door is opened it whacks the shade. This does the fitment no good whatsoever and I have replaced the light bulb with monotonous regularity.

It doesn't end there. Every time the airing cupboard door hits the light shade, it causes the whole thing to spin. After a time the wiring wears through so I have to repair it. I have done this so often that the flex has become shorter and shorter. Finally the light had migrated so far towards the ceiling, I had to replace the flex.

Mrs H refuses to get a smaller shade because: "The only sort that would let the door open is one of those round ones that fits to the ceiling, like you have in a loo! Besides it matches the one in the hall."

Then a couple of weeks ago I finally cracked. Yet again the bulb had gone. I put a new one in and that immediately blew meaning the wiring needed sorting out once again.

"That's it," I announced. "I am not repairing that light again until you get a smaller shade." Clearly Mrs H thought this was just me making another attempt to assert myself. As usual, she ignored me expecting illumination to be restored within a few days. For once she was wrong.

I knew I was gaining the upper hand when strangulated screams were coming from the airing cupboard as she groped around in the dark trying to find Brat Minor's other sock.

"For goodness sake will you mend this light!"

"Nope." I was demonstrating hitherto unseen qualities of bravado. You see, this is one of those few DIY jobs that falls within my limited sphere of capabilities. But it is something which Mrs H is reluctant to tackle.

I reckon I made her hang out for a good three weeks before her final outburst consigned the shade to redundancy and signalled a rare but sweet victory for me. The light is fixed now -

without a shade. Articles of clothing in the airing cupboard can be located and the danger of falling downstairs has been removed.

It will be sometime before I am next in a position to seriously outmanoeuvre Mrs H. I'm allowed to win the odd minor skirmish but they don't count, like the television for instance.

Remote control telly is yet to penetrate Fortress H. We still have one of those sets where old-fashioned knob twiddling is required. If the volume is too low one of us has to stagger all of six feet to turn it up. It falls to the first one to lose track of the plot to make a move.

Occasionally we can hail a passing Brat and persuade it to do the job for us. But in return we suffer barbed comments about how they suffer a social stigma at school being the only ones who have an antique telly. In fact, if they are to be believed, all their mates have a TV in their bedrooms if not satellite, cable and a video as well.

I suppose the only other area where I stand a real chance of usurping Mrs H is with the car. I know little enough about the internal combustion engine but Mrs H knows even less. She is aware where the petrol is inserted but I'm not sure if she realises it has to be paid for.

Mind you, I know very little about Mrs H's driving skills. Driving is not her favourite pastime so when we go out together it is always me behind the wheel. But a couple of weeks ago I needed to be dropped off somewhere so Mrs H drove.

We roared out of the drive as Mrs H gave it some wellie with the right foot. She went swiftly through the gears and I watched houses and hedges disappearing past me at an alarming rate. I was determined not to say anything but I must have let go a gasp or some such expression of fear.

"What!" rasped my driver.

"Oh nothing," I replied through clenched teeth. "Just wondering how many seconds the car takes to do 0 - 60."

"Hmmph," she snorted. "You can always walk." Now, I had an answer for that. It was just that I daren't say it.

Yes dear. So might you if someone doesn't keep putting petrol in.

WARM WELCOME FOR
OUR KITCHEN WIZARD

It's been mended and it's back! Once again Mrs H's beloved microwave graces the Fortress kitchen. Surgery took four weeks thanks to a delay in getting a spare part. And for four weeks Mrs H grizzled and cursed.

She stomped around waiting for things to warm through on the cooker. They would have been done in a trice in her culinary magic box. She forgot to get food out to defrost. Meals were delayed while we waited for bread to thaw. But the sun shone again in Mrs H's life when her favourite appliance was plugged in.

The treasured microwave enjoyed a homecoming of prodigal proportions. When Mrs H learnt it was coming back it was like Christmas Eve all over again. She jabbered away like an excited child expecting that special engine which would complete the train set. I wasn't there when Santa Clause from the repair shop delivered it but an ecstatic Mrs H told me all about it.

"They've even replaced the wave guard that protects the magnetron," she told me with great reverence. Realising I should be awe-struck at this I let go a low whistle of amazement. What the heck, I thought. If the return of her microwave can defrost her sufficiently to make her happy, so what? While she's content, the prospect of me being put in the stocks for something is substantially reduced.

But would you believe it? The next morning I found a saucepan of milk bubbling away on the cooker. Having pined for the wretched microwave and welcomed it home like a soldier returning from war, the idiot had forgotten it was there.

There was a time, I'm sure, when my return to Fortress H was greeted with equal warmth, particularly by my children. It wasn't that long ago that smiling faces would appear at the window when I walked up the path. I could lip read "Dad's home!" and then the faces would vanish. They would be waiting at the door attached to small breathless humans eager to give me the day's news. Nowadays there is no sign of either of them.

Recently I arrived home and had been banging around the house for a good half-hour before Brat Major surfaced. She said with a voice in which emotion was conspicuous by its absence: "Oh you're home. How long have you been here?"

Clearly she didn't care. Before I could answer she had

disappeared to perform more pressing tasks such as badgering her mother for food.

Even if I'm home first they ignore me. I was at the back door the other evening when it was flung open and two school bags were hurled at me. I just caught a perfunctory "Hi Pops," before they vanished in case they were forced into doing homework.

But I do wish I had been there to greet them a couple of Saturdays ago. They had been to the park to meet Grievous Minor, son of GBH. Remember her? My old enemy who used to live next door? Mrs H read the riot act before they went and issued a strict curfew.

"Be home at half past four. Not a minute later!" By twenty to five there was no sign of them so Mrs H activated the recovery plan. She rang GBH and of course Grievous Minor was already home. She was about to move to stage two and trigger a helicopter sweep of the village when a pair of sheepish children appeared. Their excuse was one they simply could not have made up.

"We were chased by a rotweiller," they announced. This puzzled Mrs H. Surely that should have speeded their journey home rather than delayed them. It transpired that this savage beast was in fact a harmless puppy. However, unaware of this, the brave Haversons had panicked.

Brat Major vanished through the nearest hedge leaving Brat Minor to face the animal. Our hero responded to the challenge by galvanising his little legs into saving himself from being savaged.

His sister shouted to him to join her behind the hedge. He couldn't find the gap so he tried to climb it. Furiously he scrambled away but had no more chance of scaling the hedge than he has of reaching the summit of Everest.

Then they twigged the dog wasn't interested in them. They spotted, to their embarrassment, that he was being fussed - by a lad their own age. Later they confessed that this brat-eating canine never did actually chase them.

Mrs H was quite unsympathetic pointing out that had they left the park on time the rotweiller wouldn't even have been on the scene. I did have some sympathy. Being threatened by a rotweiller must be like having the menacing GBH snapping at your heels.

I ought to behave like a rotweiller sometimes. Well, just think, that dog did something I can't do. He put fear into them. And maybe, just maybe, somebody would actually make a fuss of me.

ODD FRAGRANCE OF
A DISCO WALLFLOWER

Honestly, you'd think after all this time I'd know Mrs H pretty well. But she never ceases to confound me. Her latest effort, which left me shaking my head in bewilderment, concerned a couple of pieces of toast. The incident occurred when we arrived home from a recent PTA disco.

I must admit I was in a bit of state. Not so much because of the drink but because I spent most of the night sitting with Mrs H on one side and the old enemy from next door, GBH, on the other. Looking back, I did well to survive such intimidation. I mean, what about this for a thing to say to your husband in public?

"What's that smell?" Mrs H screwed up her nose in disgust. Then turning to me she added: "Is it you Neil?" I protested that I had washed thoroughly before coming out. And what's more I had sprayed myself liberally with a sensual potion that she herself had purchased for me.

She smelled all round me like a sniffer dog searching for drugs. The mystery was solved when the aroma was traced to my breath. The culprit was identified as some particularly spicy nibbles on the table which I had eaten.

Feeling suitably embarrassed, I was relieved when both females were invited to dance. I relaxed with my beer. Then, one of the other people at our table remarked: "Not dancing?"

"Oh no," I replied. "I shall be told when I'm required."

And so it was. Within minutes, Mrs H barked: "Neil! We'll dance to this one." After a couple of clumsy gyrations I was dismissed, only to be seized by GBH and marched back to the floor for a couple more. I thought I might get away with it, what with my smelly breath. But the effect was neutralised as by now GBH too had scoffed some spicy nibbles.

Anyway, back to the toast. I have Mrs H sussed well enough to know that when we return from a night out she is invariably hungry. To satisfy her craving for food she will usually opt for a couple of rounds of toast.

As usual, I was dispatched to make it while she exchanged gossip with our worthy Brat Warden who, amazingly, had survived her evening's duties unscathed. Now, Mrs H has strict rules about how she takes her toast. Once it pops up in the toaster it should be taken out and propped up so it doesn't' "sweat" and go soggy. Once cooled it may be buttered and served -

or so for the past twenty four years I have believed.

"This toast is cold," she complained as she buried her teeth into it.

"But that's how you have it," I rejoined indignantly.

"No I don't. Not if I'm having just butter on it. I only like it like that when I spread peanut butter or marmalade on as well." I have updated my memory banks. But I bet next time, if I serve it piping hot, it'll be wrong.

We were on the same wavelength the other night. Brat Major tried that old trick of asking me something, not getting the desired answer so asking her mother. When she got the same reply she said with contempt: "That's what Dad said."

"See how alike we are," chortled Mrs H. Before I could stop myself I'd fired off a reply.

"Cor, do you mean to say I'm irritable and shout a lot too?" Realising what I had said I braced myself for Hurricane Haverson. To my astonishment she simply chuckled. Just what is going on? I can't cope with this. She's rewriting our nuptial rulebook.

Recently I discovered that, several years ago, I did meet my perfect match. I found this out thanks to the Chinese New Year. We are in the Year of the Ox and I read one or two articles published to herald its arrival.

One was on the ancient art of Chinese astrology and included an oriental horoscope. This claims animals govern us all. Which animal depends on our dates and years of birth. For example, I am a boar - yes that is spelt correctly.

For a bit of fun I thought I'd try a birthday or two to see if, somewhere along life's M25, I'd stumbled across my ideal mate. And there she was, a rabbit. Of the boar and rabbit, the chart declared: "Opposites attract. You are almost custom made for each other."

Custom made eh? That means something that is manufactured to someone's particular specification. So my rabbit must have specified a partner who is generally inept but tries hard; is financially challenged; he's even-tempered and always eager to please; faithful and reliable. Sounds more like a Labrador than a boar.

And the rabbit? Yes you've guessed. It was, of course, Mrs H.

BRATS ASHAMED
OF THEIR "SAD" DAD

If you see Mrs H or me in the street perhaps you could reassure us that we haven't got two heads. Or an extra eye hasn't manifested itself in the middle of our foreheads. I know there must be something different about us but I'm not sure what.

The younger inmates of Fortress Haverson have always found their parents a major embarrassment. I thought it was just a phase but it seems to be getting worse. To be seen in the street with us has reached the stage of farce. We were walking along the pavement the other day when suddenly we realised Brat Major was no longer with us. She was eventually traced to a shop doorway from which she was peering furtively around.

"Coo, that was close!" she exclaimed. "Emma and Mary were on the other side of the road. They almost saw me with you."

"But look," I said with some annoyance. "Everywhere there are families shopping together. What's wrong with us?"

" It's so uncool to be out with your parents."

We do, of course, have our uses. We provide loans that rarely get repaid and unlimited free travel. I was booked to do a taxi run the other night which involved collecting Brat Major and two of her mates. Even this has rules - which I transgressed.

"Now look Dad. When they get out of the car and thank you for the lift, don't say 'It's a pleasure' like you usually do, right? "

"Why ever not?" I asked indignantly.

"It's so sad." she said disdainfully.

"What do you want me to say for goodness sake?" I thought for a moment before adding brightly: "How about 'It's cool man. Hang loose'"

"Dad! Don't you dare"

When I arrived at the collection point my daughter quietly warned me as to my conduct. However, on the journey home, I thought she was going to have a seizure. The three of them embarked on a discussion on radio stations. They all listened to Radio 1.

"My parents listen to Radio Broadland," said one of her mates. The other chum confirmed her parents did too. There followed a silence. Clearly my listening habits were needed to complete the round robin. I could feel a truculent pair of eyes focused on me, willing me to keep quiet. Finally, to break the silence, she said: "I won't tell you what my dad listens to." With that she hastily changed the subject.

I sat there feeling like some fairground freak. I was about to launch into a passionate speech about the quality of my beloved sixties music; pointing out that it can't be that bad because half the songs around today are pathetic remakes of hits from that era but we had arrived at the first dropping off point.

"Thanks for the lift."

I could feel those laser-like eyes boring into me. "No problem," I replied. There was an audible sigh of relief from the passenger seat.

The next time I was on collection duty I parked and went to meet the girls. As we headed for the car I noticed Brat Major striding purposefully ahead. I unlocked the doors and she was into the passenger seat as if she was being pursued by a raging bull.

I climbed into the car and found her poised over the radio. As soon as I turned on the ignition she swooped in a desperate bid to make sure "sad" music didn't escape from the speakers.

I do know it's not just me. I know she finds her mother equally embarrassing. She was in the car with Mrs H when, in the distance, they saw a group of boys from school. With an exclamation of "Oh no!" the truculent teenager dived below the dashboard to avoid being spotted.

They drove right beside the lads and, as Mrs H pointed out, the sight of her doing an impression of a hibernating hedgehog looked far more ridiculous than being seen with her mother.

However, I must admit that Mrs H can be an embarrassment. The other night she was at the back door calling Mystic Mog. She has always had this way of summoning cats. Regardless of how many syllables in the cat's name she splits it into two and warbles it into the night air in a kind of reverse yodel.

I would have let her carry on but for the sake of the neighbours I felt obliged to intervene. Besides, I had just passed Mystic Mog in the hall, she hadn't spotted him dart in when she opened the door. As the door starts to open he takes off. Being black and fleet of foot he's inside before you know it.

Mind you, there could be another reason why he's eager for the sanctuary of the house. Perhaps even the cat finds Mrs H embarrassing.

SWEET MEMORIES
OF TUCK SHOP TREATS

Ah me, the trials that face a young man these days. Take the hapless Brat Minor and the many daily hurdles that confront him. He grapples with such pressures as trying to find something to do when his mother shifts him from in front of the telly. Not knowing from one day to the next when he'll get pizza for tea again. And just how to con his father out of the price of a Milky Way. As if all that wasn't enough, he's found something else to worry about.

He doesn't usually read the newspaper other than to follow the footballing fortunes of his beloved Liverpool. But a few weeks ago, he caught sight of an article which has clearly had an effect on him.

It seems there is an asteroid heading towards earth. It's a chunk of rock which has parted company with a planet. Scientists have named it Toutatis. It's about three miles long and one-and-a-half miles wide. The risk of us being hit sometime in the next 25 years is quite high. Apparently three quarters of the population could be annihilated. Brat Minor churned all this over in his young mind.

"It's not fair," he complained. "I still won't be very old when it arrives."

"Well," we told our concerned son. "If it's going to happen it will. There's nothing you can do about it."

"That's all right for you," he replied indignantly. "By the time it gets here you'll have had a reasonable life." A reasonable life? What on earth did he mean by that? I pressed him on the matter.

"Well, you will have," he insisted before going on to concede: "Maybe it would have been better if you hadn't had us." He may well have a point there. Our financial position would have been vastly different. We could go up the pub at the drop of a hat and I wouldn't have a guilty conscience for depriving innocent young humans if I gobbled up the last chocolate biscuit in the tin.

Anyway, I wonder what makes him think life has been so much better for us? He and the Truculent Teenager don't do so badly. For instance, when I was at school, I had to do homework without the use of the telephone. They can't cope without making at least one call.

"I'm just going to ring Mandy about maths." Having not seen Mandy for all of two hours this provides a good excuse for a natter; not to mention a bit of a nudge in the direction of a correct answer or two.

They have loads of radio stations to chose from. I used to listen on my scratchy transistor to a fading Radio Luxembourg as the likes of Pete Murray and David Jacobs dispensed music "Brought to you by Colegate toothpaste." And do you remember the pools perms and the way the announcer emphasised parts of the address? "Horace Bachelor, Keynsham, K-E-Y-NNN-S-H-A-MMM, Keynshamm, Bristol".

Mind you, they don't have Spangles. Whatever happened to them?

"I remember Spangles," exclaimed Mrs H as we drifted down Memory Lane. "Sweets in a stripy blue and white packet." There was mint chewing gum called Beechnut that came in a little green and yellow packet. Who remembers a chocolate bar called Frys Five Boys? On the wrapper were pictures of five clean cut Beatle-like lads. And do they still make Bluebird liquorice toffees? Surely they were better than some of today's rubbish. I've seen Brat Minor's tongue assume the most hideous colour thanks to a high dosage of artificial colouring.

Let's just think about all this. If Brat Minor thinks I'm having a "reasonable life" apart from the encumbrance of him and his sister, it must mean he sees my lot with Mrs H as being reasonable.

Just wait until he gets married and has someone bossing him about. He'll discover such joys as staggering up to bed and finding a pile of papers and letters on his pillow. This is the upshot of the good woman clearing up. All he'll want to do is crawl into bed so he'll grab the heap with a view to disposing of it.

"Don't just throw them on the floor!" she'll bark. "They're there for you to sort out." He will have to learn to be cunning. To shuffle through the pile as if he is making inroads only to slip them under the bed.

He'll dig the garden only to be told he should have painted the guttering. The night he stops after work to have a pint with his mates will be the night she decides to cook something special.

If the car breaks down on her it'll be his fault. She'll moan at him because she's never got the right outfit for the occasion and when she asks him what he thinks of her new clothes, whatever he says will be wrong.

If he can survive that lot, I'm sure he can handle any asteroid.

MEMORIES OF
THE SCAM OF '73

We've just gone through the 24th pain barrier in years of wedded bliss. Throughout this period of penal servitude I have always believed I got away with a cunning ploy when we fixed the date of our wedding.

My illusion was shattered only a month or so a go. I was scanning our hockey fixture card and, foolishly, admitted to Mrs H that Saturday April 5th read "No game". However, a match was subsequently arranged. So having announced that I would not be partaking in the one period of recreation I am allowed each week, I had to throw myself on her mercy and beg for clemency. Magnanimously, she let me out to play.

The significant thing about all this is, that on the corresponding Saturday 24 years ago, our fixture list also read "No game". Now, the then Miss H had targeted the previous week, March 31st, for the formal attachment of the ball and chain. I consulted the fixture card and spun her a yarn that an extra week would give us a bit longer to make all the arrangements and the wedding was moved to April 7th.

Well, I heard her on the 'phone three or four weeks ago, just after I had been given clearance to play on April 5th. "Yes," she said scornfully. "He's got a game now so he won't be here." Then she went on to reveal that all along she's known the truth about the scam I pulled in 1973. "Course you know, they didn't have a game on the day we got married. I wonder what he'd have done then if they'd suddenly fixed up a match."

Having discovered she's perhaps not as daft as I thought, I have to say there remain plenty of occasions when I have cause to doubt her sanity. For instance, recently I have stumbled across a couple of her famous aide memoirs. Those notes that she leaves around the house to remind her and the rest of us of the multitude of tasks that need to be done to keep Fortress Haverson ticking over. The first was a note aimed at me.

She was out when I arrived home from work so awaiting me were the usual series of instructions. Heaven forbid that I should be left to my own devices. Among the prompts was one requesting: "Please get the washing in". Nothing strange in that except she had signed it with her Christian name. Why? She's never done that before. Did she think the neighbour might also leave a chit asking me to get the washing in so she needed to make it clear which line had to be cleared?

The other memory jogger was a real corker. It was a note to herself. "Have I got plastic spoon in car boot?" Well what do you make of that one? I refused to ask and spent a good couple of weeks trying to come up with a rational explanation. The best I could manage was that she had got into the habit of stopping in a lay-by on the way back from the supermarket to consume yoghurt. Or perhaps she's a closet Pot Noodle eater and takes a flask of hot water with her to gobble a roadside snack.

Finally, I just had to satisfy my curiosity. It turned out my Pot Noodle theory wasn't too wide of the mark but she has been unable to explain why the car boot should be a likely place to search for a plastic spoon.

Rather than seek professional help for her, I gave her the benefit of the doubt. After all, she does carry so much rubbish around in the boot of the car. The other day I spotted a cardboard box full of containers of various sizes being unloaded. There was a bucket, an ice cream carton, a bowl, a jelly mould and several other similar receptacles. What on earth had she been up to? This time I just had to ask.

She had used them at school to help a small group of children learn about capacity. The lesson consisted of a discussion on the units of measurement, litres and millilitres. This is all backed up by a bit of practical work, hence Mrs H's visual aids.

Using a jug, they poured water into the containers to estimate how much each held. Following the demonstration, Mrs H tested their understanding of litres and millilitres.

"So," she asked, "What do we measure liquids in?" Without a moments hesitation they answered in one voice.

"A jug Mrs Haverson."

At least it's not just me.

THE DAY MRS H LET POWER
GO TO HER ED

It began as just another average weekend. Being Saturday, we were allowed a short lie-in before we were rallied into playing our respective parts in another well-oiled Fortress day. Even my monthly visit to the crimper followed its normal course.

She snipped busily away muttering that I really should take the bold step and have the Haverson barnet redesigned, a task that she would be happy to perform. As usual I withdrew into my unadventurous shell, politely refusing this golden opportunity to acquire a new image with my standard excuse that such dramatic measures could only be executed with specific authorisation from Mrs H.

So with the standard trim having been applied to my hair, I fled the crimper. Before heading home I speculated a moderate amount on the lottery which was to see me achieve a Fortress record of two numbers that matched those thrown out by that wretched machine.

I arrived home to find the younger inmates being told by a vociferous Mrs H that they really didn't need to be watching television at that time on a Saturday morning. Having said that, Mrs H was drinking coffee and reading the paper; one of those rare moments when she is practically motionless.

And then the phone rang and the pace of Fortress life changed altogether.

"Mum! It's Uncle Ed for you," yelled Brat Major. Ed is Mrs H's American cousin. In this country on business, he planned to visit Fortress Haverson. Mrs H went straight into overdrive.

"Ed's coming tomorrow afternoon," she babbled. "Just look at the state of this place. I'll have to go through the house today. We're out most of tomorrow." She always gets hyper about the housework if visitors are expected. I fully expect her to twizzle round in a blur and reappear in a caped outfit with a big H on the front as...Hooverwoman!

"I'll need your help," she wailed. Brat Minor immediately did his Lord Lucan and didn't materialise until the heat had died down. Brat Major found herself heading to the north wing with a duster and clear instructions to "move the ornaments and dust them carefully."

"Neil," she barked. "Do the stairs and get right in the corners. That's where it collects." Just what "it" was, I couldn't wait to find out.

Driven relentlessly on by Hooverwoman we did our best to make Fortress H guest-worthy. Of course this was Saturday and Ed wasn't due until later on Sunday so we had to pad carefully round the place for twenty-four hours in case we messed anything up. Fortunately we had arranged to see some relatives on Sunday so we wouldn't be there to create any dust.

Chatting to our relatives took the focus off the house but the attention was turned on me. It always amazes me how she can be in the middle of pontificating when suddenly something about me grabs her attention and just has to be said.

"Well, I said to her the best thing to do is...Neil! What socks have you got on? They're awful. Pull the legs of your trousers down and cover them up." Now, I can tell you, it's no easy task to assume a normal sitting position while trying to maximise the length of your trouser legs.

Apart from a couple of barbed comments about the shape of my stomach being a direct result of my posture, she left me alone for a while. Then, all of a sudden: "You've got one collar out of your jumper and one in. Either have them both out or both in."

This is a no win situation. Whichever way I chose to have my collar will be wrong. "No. I prefer them both in. That looks feminine."

Just as I thought there wasn't much left of me to have a go at, she came out with the most staggering statement of all.

"When did you last have your hair cut?"

"Actually it was a little over 24 hours ago."

"Well, comb it. You've lost your parting." Crimper, please note. This confirms that a restyle will only be possible if a planning application is submitted well in advance to Mrs H.

Having been through her mincer all afternoon, I wondered what lay in store for me when Ed arrived. But surely he wouldn't have time to listen to criticism of me. He'd be too busy with his clipboard inspecting the standard of the housework.

I opened the door to the tall, broad shouldered Ed. He grasped my modest hand in his cavernous fist, gave Hooverwoman a crushing hug and sat down to eat. Clearly he was going to wait until after the meal before running his eye over the stairs to see if I had got "it" out of the all the corners.

He didn't. Instead he disappeared with Brat Minor to play basketball. There was no mention of housework at all. Mrs H remained mellow and the evening went rather well.

Mind you, I had changed my socks.

EAR BASHING OVER
MY SPUD MASHING

There are one or two sceptics who hold the view that Mrs H is much maligned by me. They harbour opinions that she cannot possibly be as I portray her. In spite of recounting endless examples of the way Fortress H and its inmates are driven through life by the good lady, I am unable to shake these beliefs.

Occasionally someone is brave enough to come forward with a comment which I can take down and use in evidence.

It was at the school fete the other Saturday that confirmation of Mrs H's ability to talk was provided. She was helping with the refreshments while I was supposed to be looking after our car boot stall. I managed to persuade Brat Major to take over while I went in search of a hot dog. On the way I met a friend and fellow car booter who had also slipped his leash.

"Just seen Mrs H," he said. "Met her when I was going into the toilet." Now, here is the clincher. "Er..she's not the best person to bump into when you're desperate for the loo." He delivered this damning bit of evidence while demonstrating the tension of his experience by shuffling from foot to foot.

It must have been my lucky day. When I returned to the car we finally sold the chipper. The chipper has accompanied us to at least three car boot sales only to be brought back home for a further spell in the loft before the next outing.

It is an evil looking device designed for converting the raw potato into chips. Insert the potato, push the handle down hard and watch as the spud is forced through a grid, slicing it into perfect chips. Sounds simple but we have produced some peculiar shaped chips and sustained many a sore knuckle.

Half way through the day just as Brat Major suggested removing it as unsaleable a chap wandered by, tenderly picked up the chipper and studied it like a piece of Royal Doulton.

"How much?" he asked. I could barely suppress the excitement in my voice as I asked a highly speculative price.

"Seventy five pence?" I stammered optimistically. To my astonishment he reached in his pocket and produced the money. He walked away smiling happily. Did he know something I didn't know? Maybe it was destined for the Science Museum.

My luck got even better. Yet more evidence of Mrs H and her ways presented itself. This time it was paying testament to how organised she is. A member of the PTA came up and in the course of conversation mentioned that when she arrived to prepare the refreshments she discovered she had forgotten to bring some rubber gloves.

"Then your wife walked in and I thought good old Mrs H. Sure enough she had her Marigolds with her."

I wish one of those who doubt my profiles of Mrs H had been there the other night to hear the almost evangelical address I received on mashed potato. Yes, seriously. I was subjected to a short sharp lecture on pulping root vegetables.

I was ordered to assist with the evening meal. This involves keeping the washing up going, chopping vegetables with a knife upon whose blade you could ride to Yarmouth and back without fear of a laceration, and mashing the potatoes.

"Who mashed the potatoes?" Mrs H demanded accusingly. As I was the only one in the kitchen it didn't take a masterstroke of deduction to identify the culprit. "It's lumpy. They won't eat it."

"You always complain my mash is lumpy. Don't get me to mash the potatoes in future."

"Don't be so silly! You're such a defeatist. You should keep mashing potatoes until you get it right. Do it again and again. Keep mashing and mashing and mashing until you get it nice and fluffy." She was starting to get worked up now. I listened for the sound of a celestial choir. But all I heard was the more earthly sound of a hungry Brat whinging for its food. I would add that said brat and its sibling consumed my mash without complaint.

It seems that there is always something to learn. I wandered into the bedroom the other day as Mrs H was making the bed. Thinking I was being helpful I grabbed one side of the duvet and helped pull it into position.

"Pull it right up. Come on pull, pull, pull! I like it so it goes under your chin when you snuggle down." Even as I write, there has just been a hysterical cry form the top of the stairs.

"Arrrrggh! Neil! Just look how you've put that pile of shirts in the airing cupboard. If I touch them the whole lot will collapse."

It's a hard life. But at least I can go to the loo when Mrs H is talking. She just bawls at me through the door.

ATTENTION!
THIS IS MRS H SPEAKING

I have a message for a sales assistant in a well-known city department store. You just don't know how lucky you are. A few days ago she was that much from being savaged. But Mrs H changed her mind and decided not to complain.

This girl's great escape came to light when I recounted to Mrs H an incident I had found rather amusing. Clutching my Mrs H list, I was in this particular store desperately trying to unload some money when there was an announcement over the loudspeaker system.

"Visit the bra department. There you will be measured by one of our highly trained bra advisers and entered in our prize draw." What, I wondered, qualified one for entry into the draw? Did you have to be a certain cup size?

I found myself grinning all the way up the escalator. I could just hear the result being announced. "And the winner of the 42 B draw is Mrs Mabel Chesterton of Wiggenhall."

On arrival at Fortress Haverson that evening I shared this moment with Mrs H. Now, I can always tell when she has something to say. While I am still telling my story she serves notice that she is about to make a speech by sucking in a good supply of oxygen. Her face takes on that look of an opera singer about to burst into a taxing aria. Then, as soon as I finish speaking - sometimes before - she lets fly.

"Do you know, I hadn't noticed them making announcements before! But I was in there the other day and I found it really intrusive. In fact I was so annoyed I was going to complain to the assistant. But I just didn't have the time."

Just imagine this hapless employee going about her work when a hurricane in the form of Mrs H blows up. I suspect Mrs H in rampant complaining mode would have well outperformed any set of loudspeakers. Besides what the assistant could have done about it, I really don't know.

"I'm so sorry madam. I'll go and switch it off so they can't use it."

I did find it a little comforting that Mrs H found the irritating. Whilst a Mrs H bellow can penetrate to the remotest corner of Fortress Haverson - the neighbours can testify to that - just think what life would be like if she installed such a system to assist her in dispensing her orders and motivating us to carry them out.

Picture Mrs H in her command bunker. Posted on the wall are details of jobs to be done. On the table is a scale plan of Fortress H with cardboard models of me and my fellow inmates which Mrs H moves into position as she directs us around the house to carry out our tasks.

"Good afternoon. This is a Fortress announcement. Would all inmates kindly assemble in the kitchen where their evening meal is about to be prepared." There'd be no escape.

"Good evening. It is now 8.30 p.m. would the younger inmates please report to the bathroom for teeth cleaning and final ablutions. And don't whinge!" She could even reach me in the loft.

"Neil? Are you listening to me? I know you can hear me. There's a spider in the bathroom. Please remove it."

You know, I do wonder sometimes what life would be like if I didn't have Mrs H in the engine room. If she's goes out I find I go through a flat patch before I can galvanise myself into some sort of action. It's rather like that feeling when you come out of a disco after a couple of hours of throbbing music and flashing lights. Suddenly you realise certain senses have been numbed.

During this period of tranquillity I tend to potter around aimlessly. It's only when I realise I will be expected to provide evidence that I have been gainfully employed that I get stuck in.

I have sailed close to the wind here and left it a bit late. There are one or two tricks I have up my sleeve for when a slam of the car door heralds Mrs H's arrival home.

A good wheeze is to have the toolbox open with a screwdriver or two scattered randomly about the place. And making use of the garage light is another cunning ploy.

"Did you know the garage light is on?" asks Mrs H as she comes in.

"Oh damn! I must have forgotten to switch it off when I put the extension light away." That's enough to sew the seed in her mind that I have been grafting in some dark corner of Fortress H.

I wonder if she thinks like this when she hears me coming home from work. Does she panic because she hasn't got tea ready? I doubt it. She's probably laying in wait to announce my evening duties over her public address system.

A FINE DISPLAY
BY KITCHEN TEAM

I was tidying up the garden. Nearby a car started and made its way up the road. This was the only sign of any other human activity in the neighbourhood. Except for one other thing. Yes you've guessed it. From the kitchen of Fortress Haverson came the sound of another episode in the never-ending drama of Her Truculence versus Mrs H.

I couldn't help wondering why so much of home life is lived in the kitchen? It seems that people do tend to congregate there. Well, I suppose the lounge is more of a grown ups playroom where we read, entertain, watch TV and tolerate the children. The bedroom is hardly the place to hold a family conference. And as for the garden, well, Mrs H only goes there to hang out the washing.

Certainly, at Fortress Haverson, the kitchen is the nerve centre. For Mrs H it is the command module from which she directs operations. This draws the rest of us to it like moths to light so it has become the place where family crisis are solved, life is debated and decisions made. Amid the washing up and cooking some riveting topics come on to the agenda.

"How much would I get paid for cutting the grass?" demanded the impecunious Brat Minor the other evening.

"I'd have to see how long the grass was," I replied. The young gardener looked puzzled. Mrs H supplied the answer for him

"It's harder to cut when it's longer," she interjected.

"Your mother," I said with great precision, "does not speak from personal experience."

"I have no desire to mow the lawn," she replied haughtily. "Anyway, I don't see you in here baking."

We were boiling up for a good old bout of point scoring. These battles provide great Brat entertainment but this time they were to be disappointed. The conversation came to a natural halt, as we had to shuffle round to allow Mrs H to continue uninhibited the pull towards the common good. You see, the Fortress kitchen is not very big so when we are all in there cat swinging is at a premium.

When these forums emerge, tools get downed to make for full concentration on the matter in hand - except in the case of the perpetually active Mrs H. And you can bet your life that wherever I have rested on my laurels, I'm in Mrs H's way; usually in front of the fridge when she suddenly has the need to extract an aubergine.

We have all become adept at getting a drink and threading our way through the "crowd" without spilling it. And when Mrs H has organised us all into helping with a meal we perform like a motor cycle display team. Our star turn is kicked started when Mrs H cries: "Put the veg on!" We head in different directions clutching saucepans, fresh carrots and frozen peas. Without a word being spoken we weave our way in and out culminating in a grand finale as our respective saucepans make it to the cooker without discharging the contents over a fellow inmate.

But recently Mrs H threw in a wobbly and the well-honed routines were reduced to chaos.

The cutlery drawer has been in the wrong place for 16 years. It's the opposite end of the kitchen to the sink which means that when I'm washing up I have to snake my way past the other galley slaves to put my shining knives and forks away.

Of course, we've always intended to swap things around but, like everything else, we never got round to it. Anyway we are so used to where it is that you could blindfold any of us and I guarantee we could locate the drawer and unerringly extract that fork with the bent tines.

Then without notice, Mrs H moved it to the other end of the kitchen. She added a further complication by using a new tray with compartments which bore no resemblance to the old one. So once we had found the right drawer we still had to home in on the correct piece of cutlery.

Just as we were readjusting, Mrs H struck again. She wasn't happy with the relocation so she moved the cutlery to the next drawer. Now it was taking up to three attempts to get a teaspoon. There was a noticeable amount of drawer slamming followed by outbursts of violent cursing as we bumped into one another returning from aborted cutlery hunts.

"Am I keeping you on your toes," asked Mrs H with a quite unnecessary amount of pleasure. Her next remark was clearly directed at me. "It's good for you when you get older to move things around. It helps keep your mind sharp."

Oh really? I wonder if that's the reason I can never find any money about the place.

FLEAS HOP ABOARD
THE PARK AND RIDE

I peered out of the window into the gloom. Daylight was fast disappearing but on the patio I could make out a large shape. I could see the shape was gently heaving. Gradually, as my eyes adjusted to the light, I realised that the shape was composed of two people. One was Her Truculence, sitting cross-legged on the concrete. Clamped in her lap was Mystic Mog, the Fortress Mouse-catcher.

Completing the shape was Mrs H. The movement that I had spotted was Mrs H raking systematically through her beloved mog's fur. Suddenly the two of them sprung apart.

"There's one!" went up the cry. "Quick get him, get him." Pandemonium broke out. A startled mog clawed his way to freedom as two hysterical females appeared to be attempting to stamp out an imaginary fire.

Mystic Mog has made it to his first birthday. My efforts to make his spell on the payroll temporary have failed. He has wheedled his way into the affections of those that matter and I have conceded defeat. But at the moment he is not popular. He has fleas. Not just ordinary fleas. Oh no, these are some species of super flea. What I was witnessing in the twilight on the patio was Mrs H and her daughter trying to exterminate the little blighters.

So far they have resisted all anti-flea treatments. Much to his displeasure, the mog has been sprayed with a potent brew that Mrs H got from the vet. His box has been sprayed, even sections of carpet have received a dousing but the army of fleas marches on. The irony of it all is, that the only person affected is the mog's greatest supporter, Mrs - "he's a dear little chap" - H.

She has been bitten unmercifully about the legs and really has suffered some discomfort. I came home one night to such wailing I thought I had walked into an Indian Reservation. I followed the sound of the painful chanting and discovered Mrs H in the hall jigging around like a demented Apache.

Mrs H intensified her campaign to eliminate the flea. This consisted of relentless vacuuming to suck the eggs from their refuge in the carpet. The vacuum bag was sprayed with insecticide so that any little flea that thought he was going on a mystery tour would suffer acute travel sickness. Mrs H even connected the hose to the vacuum cleaner and tried Hoovering the mog but he resisted almost as much Brat Minor does when he is made to wash his hair.

The situation did not improve so Mrs - "he's adorable" - H sought expert advice. This came in the form of a leaflet entitled: "Understanding Fleas".

What was she up to now? Was she studying to become a flea psychiatrist? Perhaps she was hoping to counsel the wretched things and persuade them that there is more to life than living on a cat and getting their kicks out of biting his mistress.

The leaflet turned out to be promoting yet another flea eradicator. But it made good reading. It detailed, with illustrations, the life cycle of the flea. I am now an expert.

To get into the house, they use the cat as a kind of park and ride. They hop aboard the mog and are transported indoors. Having set up home in his fur they lay eggs at the rate of 30 a day.

Then, thanks to the likes of Mrs - "he's a little sweetie" - H playing silly games with the mog, the eggs are dislodged and roll off into the carpet where they hatch into larvae. If they survive Mrs - "look at his little face" - H and her marauding vacuum cleaner they spin a cocoon and wait until a cat passes by. Once again they leap on board and start the whole cycle again.

They will languish in their cocoons for months waiting for a cat to arrive. I bet two then turn up at once.

Throughout it all the one least affected seems to be the mog himself. With the exception of attempted Hoovering and being subjected to noxious sprays, he has gone about his daily routines undeterred.

I must say he has proved to be a couple of chunky morsels short of a full tin. He doesn't do everything that normal cats do. On balmy summer evenings he can be seen almost cart-wheeling round the garden. He is indulging in his favourite pursuit of catch the midge. He leaps and twists around the lawn like a deranged gymnast. Occasionally he'll capture a sluggish gnat and crunch his way through a winged snack.

I wonder sometimes how I stick all this. I've two children that I continually embarrass, I have a wife that...well, you know all about her and now we have a psychotic cat. In comparison the flea doesn't lead too bad a life.

Now there's a thought. I wonder how you spin a cocoon

ALL DRESSED UP
FOR A DRESSING DOWN

Be positive with your children, the experts say. If you tell them they're no good at things they'll begin to believe it themselves. Whilst I understand the point being made, I can only assume the so-called experts that said this don't have children.

I've tried, believe me I've tried. I praise the little dears when they do well and encourage them when things don't go quite according to plan. But there are occasions when I lose sight of the point. For instance, the other evening I glanced out of the window just in time to see a compact disc whiz past. I sought out the perpetrator of this flying saucer. It was the male brat.

Try as I might, I could find nothing positive or encouraging to say to him. Especially when he justified his actions with the explanation: "It makes a good Frisbee." Instead my speech was riddled with words like "stupid" and "idiot" and "I cannot believe I fathered you."

Of course this policy of edification does not just apply to children. Even me, the faithful old retainer, likes to be encouraged and praised. But last week, I locked antlers with Mrs H in a similar way to my encounter with Brat Minor over his CD. We were getting ready to go out for a pub meal with some friends.

Mrs H was in full ball gown choosing mode. Clothes of differing length, colour, weight and age were spread around the bedroom like a jumble sale. We had the "What tights shall I wear?" speech. This is the one that goes: "It's too hot for tights really but my legs are so pale! Can't wear dark tights in the summer, ought to wear light tights but they don't look right with any of these." Then the killer: "What do you think?"

I opted for the old flattery technique. "Nothing wrong with your legs," I asserted. This was enough to side-track her and she spent the next couple of minutes telling me how horrible they were.

Time was running out. She had narrowed her choice of outfit down to just three. There was a wail of horror and I thought the favoured ensemble was about to be eliminated. "Oh no! This dress needs ironing."

But suddenly it was back as an option. Motivated by a desire to get to the pub before last orders I heard myself saying: "I'll have a go if you like."

With the cry of "Don't have the iron too hot," ringing in my ears I headed downstairs. Carefully I pressed the dress and took it back to its owner.

"Oh you haven't ironed it yet then." she said sarcastically. "When I said don't have the iron too hot I meant hotter than that!" Note the lack of praise for my efforts.

While she was in the bath I had another go. As I grafted the truculent teenager wandered into the room. I thought a heavy sigh followed by a pitiful "I hope I'm doing this OK," might stimulate some sympathy.

I waited for "Here Dad, give me the iron. I'll do that" but she remained unmoved.

I finished my pressing and dived in the bath before Mrs H could inspect my latest effort. It was after I had cleansed myself that I got into trouble.

Mrs H came into the bathroom and prepared to insert her contact lenses. As she was playing with all her solutions I set about squirting something manly and sensual under my armpits. The first hiss of spray caused Mrs H to go into meltdown.

"Stop!" she yelled, "Don't do that! It'll get on my lenses and damage them." Obediently I leapt out of the bathroom door before treating the other armpit. However, hearing the second squirt, a half blind Mrs H hurled herself out of the bathroom and began berating me for ignoring her pleas and continuing to spray.

"But...but...," I protested. "I got out as soon as you shouted."

"Oh," she said. "I thought you were still in the bathroom." Could there be an apology coming? Alas no, she returned to the attack. "So you mean to say I ran out of the bathroom and caught the second lot of deodorant as well?" It was, of course, all my fault but fortunately no harm was done and her vision was good enough to inspect the quality of my ironing.

She put the dress on. It appeared my efforts had not been in vain. But then she asked the full length mirror to confirm her choice. "Oh I can't wear this with these sandals." With that the dress that I had so meticulously ironed was flung on the bed.

Finally, she was as satisfied as any woman ever is with their appearance. But she hadn't done with me yet. She wheeled round and pointing accusingly at me said: "It's no good. I shall have to get some new shoes."

Yes dear. Just make sure they go with your legs.

MOG'S THE CREAM
OF FORTRESS H

Following my whinge a couple of weeks ago that Fortress H has a four-legged colony of fleas in the form of Mystic Mog, advice has been plentiful as to how we might exterminate them. More sprays have been suggested together with capsules, powders and a substance to put in the mog's food. My favoured option remains unchanged. Get rid of the fleas' mode of transport.

What surprised me was the effect my words had on some cat owners. There are those of you that were moved to give your pet's bedding a good wash or a spray. One friend whose cat hadn't got fleas became overwhelmed with the urge to scratch just at thought of it.

In spite of her itchy legs, Mrs H continues to dote on "the dear little chap". The other evening there she sat on the settee smiling sloppily at the bag of fleas curled up in her lap.

"You know he is a dear little fella," she said. "He's not like any other cat we've had. He doesn't make a fuss when he wants his food. He just looks up at me with appealing little eyes."

"I wonder where he gets that from?" I asked pointedly. Mrs H looked at me in surprise. Then the penny dropped. "Yes," I continued when I realised she had joined me on the same wavelength. "The difference is the mournful look works for him, it doesn't for me. And I don't give you fleas." But I was wasting my words. There is a lot of stony ground at Fortress H.

Meanwhile the mog continues to demonstrate that, when it comes to matters of the brain, someone has pressed his "paws" button.

In all that rain we had recently I found him sheltering - under a garden bench with a slatted seat. And when he has finished eating he goes through the motions of covering his food up as if he has just used his litter.

Mind you, I did think he had kick-started his instincts when I came home one evening to find a dead bird on the patio. The mog was in the vicinity prowling around menacingly but for some reason keeping a degree of concrete between him and the deceased bird.

"Has he done it?" I enquired as I crossed the threshold of Fortress H. "Has he bagged his first prey?"

"Oh no," said Mrs H with unusual contempt. "The poor bird flew into the window and died. The mog just ignored it."

I made a few derogatory remarks but all to no avail. The mog continues to be in favour and my place in the Fortress hierarchy remains slightly lower than below stairs. In fact recently my standing was highlighted in public.

We went to an evening at the High School to learn more about what faces Her Truculence over the next two years as she prepares for her GCSEs. Probably more to the point, how much effort with the carrot and stick will be required from us to push her through the work.

If current performance is anything to go by, I can't say I'm looking forward to it. As she grows up I suspect Mrs H and I will age rapidly. It's the same old problem of getting her to do her homework.

Yes, there is a diary we have to sign. But she waits until the morning she has to hand it in it before thrusting it under my nose just as I'm leaving for work with the demand: "Sign this will you?"

"Have you done it all? I haven't seen it." This prompts a run down of the subjects.

"Done that, done that. Mum saw the history and English. You saw me doing my art. And French doesn't have to be in until Friday. I don't understand the maths so I'm not doing that."

"I'm not signing it then if all I've seen is the art. Go and get the rest and show me."

"I can't. I've handed it in." I don't know why she does this because when pushed the truculent one invariably manages to produce evidence of academic achievement and I sign the diary.

Anyway, the evening at the school was divided into four sessions with a range of subjects at each one. As there were no clashes of subjects at the first two we decided I would go only to the latter sessions. We indicated this on the form. On the evening a four-page sheet was handed out allocating parents to subjects for each session.

Now, as I was not attending the first two, you would have thought for those ones, my name would have been left off the list. However, it appears my station in society is more than apparent.

At the bottom of pages 1 and 2, following all the subject headings and parents names was a single heading with one name standing proud underneath. "Unallocated. Mr Haverson".

Doesn't that just sum it all up?

TELLING IT STRAIGHT
FROM A DISTANCE

As we bowled along in the car, conversation ground to halt so I thought I'd liven things up a bit. "I saw the most appalling sight in the village yesterday," I said. This grabbed their attention. "Yes," I went on, "I saw a father out...well he was...he was out cycling with his son." Mrs H sucked in a sharp breath and joined in the wind-up.

"And do you know what? Your daughter rang to invite a friend round yesterday but she couldn't come because she was going shopping with...wait for it...her mother." Yes it was the old embarrassment kick again but this time I was making a point.

We are not in Brat Minor's good books at the moment because we won't let him cycle any great distance on his own. This is due simply to the fact that last time I cycled with him he was a liability. He made full use of the road, so much so that there wasn't much tarmac left for any one else. Except when he came to a parked car. Here he seemed to set himself the challenge of riding past the vehicle, getting as close to it as possible without gouging the paintwork with his handlebars.

This was a good couple of years ago but these days he is so embarrassed to be seen with me that he refuses to let me ride with him. Admittedly this is due partly to my old bike which dates only slightly later than the penny farthing.

With all this agro to contend with as well as everything else I have to put up with I am grateful for any help. My thanks to a sympathetic correspondent from Matlaske who from time to time sends me helpful hints to sustain life at Fortress Haverson. The latest dispatch consisted of an extract from a magazine which gives the experts' views on how to survive the truculent years.

It's all very well setting it down on paper but putting it into practice is a different kettle of fish ("Oh no not fish! I hate fish it's disgusting!" - Her Truculence unbonding with her mother over what Mrs H considers a healthy diet).

For example, the experts say it is not good to fight in front of your children. If you do, you should make sure they see you resolve it. Apparently this signals that you are really a cohesive team.

No problem here. Our rows last only as long as it takes me to capitulate.

One expert asserts that teenagers need privacy; you should

give them some space. Ideally this should be their bedroom. Keep out of it; don't even clean it. With Brat Minor's squat that is no problem. It is in such a disgusting state that entry is tortuous at the best of times. And as for the Truculent Teenager, well, if Mrs H didn't rescue clothes from her daughter's room now and again, the young fashion guru would never have any clean things to wear.

Make time to listen to your teenager, is another thought. That's fine if they'll talk in the first place. The times I've seen a red faced Mrs H with her nose inches from her daughter's bellowing: "Speak to me! I'm not a mind reader. How do I know what you're thinking if you won't say anything."

In fact, at times like this, it is quite easy to read the truculent mind. Her body language says it all. "For goodness sake leave me alone. Neighbours is on and I really don't need to have a reason for thumping my brother."

There was an intriguing suggestion of how to get round the problem of the little darlings not listening. Make a tape of what you want to say. But I wonder how you would get them to listen to it. I suppose it would have to be muddled up among their music collections.

I have this wonderful image of the Truculent Teenager on a school trip. There they are aboard the coach and on goes the Walkman. Just picture her face when the tape starts.

"Hello, this is your father speaking. When I was pursuing you round the house the other night I was trying to discuss with you one or two things that have, well, to be frank, upset your mother. She was very hurt at your blunt refusal to eat any of your Aubergine Bake. We know everybody else in your class, in fact in the whole school, lives on cheeseburgers, chips and Coke but your mother is only concerned about...what's that dear? I'm recording a message for your daughter. Yes I know your washing needs to come in if it's raining.

"Oh look I'll have to talk to you when you get home. Your mother wants me to...yes, yes all right dear. I'm coming!"

Perhaps I should use this idea myself. Just think communicating with Mrs H and she can't answer back.

BLOOD SPILLED AFTER
A MINOR ACCIDENT

It started as tummy ache. It finished up as "Waves of pain" and had Brat Minor writhing in agony. We reacted like typical parents. First we administered the "Come on old chap. It'll soon pass" Then as time wore on and the pain got worse we took more interest. What had he had eaten? Had he been to the loo?

Between wails we established that he had consumed the same as the rest of us and his digestive system was operating normally so it must be something else. Then we hit that stage when you suddenly realise something serious may be wrong and a touch of panic creeps in.

Mrs H phoned the doctor and described the symptoms. He diagnosed colic, prescribed Paracetomol and said that if there was no improvement he would pay us a visit. And then Mrs H came out with one of her classics.

"If the doctor does have to come out, I better give the place a quick dust." Honestly! As if Medicine Man would be interested in the state of Fortress Haverson.

"Give him these tablets three times a day before meals, keep him warm and make sure you vacuum the hall."

Poor old Brat Minor continued to roll around on the sofa. It was as if it was connected to the mains and someone threw the switch every few seconds sending a mighty charge through his bony little body.

Medicine Man was summoned. He waded through the dust and examined his patient. He prodded various areas of the squirming Brat Minor's anatomy blissfully unaware that it is not known when those parts were last brought into contact with soap.

The original diagnosis was confirmed and strong painkillers prescribed. Medicine Man then asked if he could wash his hands to purge them of the experience of touching the exposed regions of his unsavoury patient. However, he fell victim to the Haversons playing their game of seeing who will crack first and get a new bar of soap out of the cupboard.

The soap Mrs H buys has a label on it. We had eked it out so much that by the time the doc got to use it, virtually the only bit left was the label. Goodness knows what tales he took back to the surgery, what with all that dust as well.

Eventually Brat Minor showed signs of recovery but clearly

was going to be denied attending his seat of learning the following day. "I better give GBH a quick ring and tell her we won't be at school tomorrow." Another classic! Mrs H and GBH, that ex-neighbour of ours, having a quick phone call is about as likely as me going to the pub for a heavy night on the orange juice.

These two women gossiping is bad enough but when the subject is illness there was no holding them. I wouldn't say the doctor's diagnosis was questioned but they trawled through practically every decease known to man and ruminated on which of their acquaintances had contracted which ailment.

And something must have been lost in the translation because the next day Grievous Minor announced to his mates that Brat Minor was suffering from cholera

Now oddly enough, the following weekend GBH unwittingly played a part in healing me. I sustained an injury in the execution of a typical example of "don't do as I do, do as I say". Having spent years lecturing the younger inmates on the need for care with the bread knife, I was attempting a suicidal slicing of the end of a loaf which was wobbling around like a blancmange.

Of course the inevitable happened. As I sawed away the bread crumpled and I hacked into my finger. With a shriek prompted more by shock than pain I flung down the knife and headed for the bathroom.

As I stood there pumping blood my family rallied round. I could hear Mrs H organising things.

"Quick! Grab a cloth." Ah, help was on the way. Or was it? "Look there's blood on the carpet, some on the cupboard door. It's on the wall. Honestly he's got it everywhere!" Thanks! There I was, haemorrhaging furiously and they were more concerned with the mess. Finally Mrs H appeared.

"Hmm," she said examining the damage. "I'm not trained in first aid. I may have to ring GBH and get her to come round." Immediately the bleeding stopped. All it took was the threat of a visit from GBH and my blood was panicked into clotting.

Bandaged up, I was put on light duties. But after a couple of days my input to the common good of Fortress H was being missed - mainly in the washing up department.

In spite of my protestations I was summoned for a wound inspection before being pressed back into service. Mrs H studied my finger carefully.

"Hmm. It's healing all right. Mind you, you'll have a scar. You won't heal so well now, you know. You're old."

DON'T TURN YOUR BACK
ON PARSLEY

All right lads, hands up all those who think they know how to grill bacon. Thought so. Well I bet you're not doing it properly. I thought I could perform this simple task but Mrs H was forced to school me in the art of what I can only describe as formation grilling.

It started with "I could do with a hand with the meal tonight." This throwaway line is her way of making me a kitchen conscript - and it's non-negotiable. Even so a flood of words came to my lips. "But I've got the car to clean, the lawn to mow, the garden to dig. I was going to bond with my son and do chaps' things." They got as far as my lips but when they came out they were compressed into two words: "Yes dear".

I was given the bacon to grill - mustn't fry it, too much fat, bad for you. As there was too much to spread across the grill I began overlapping it as I thought I had been told. A huge "Tcchh!" in my ear that sounded like two hippos kissing alerted me to the fact that I was doing something wrong.

"No, no. You lay it alternately with the wide bit of the first rasher at the bottom then the next piece has the wider bit at the top. And you've started from the wrong end of the grill pan. The fat of the next piece of bacon is supposed to overlay the meat of the previous bit. You've got it the other way round." Now I hope you all understood that.

There's no point in me arguing because Mrs H rules the roost. If ever this was in doubt, confirmation came courtesy of a piece of parsley. Weeks ago, Mrs H appeared with a sprig of parsley in a pot. It soon outgrew its home and I was asked to find a place for it in the garden.

Well, a chap has other things on his mind and my priorities did not include the well being of a bit of parsley. But Mrs H wore me down. Nearly all communications between the two of us ended with "And you still haven't planted that parsley."

Eventually it took on a rather sickly appearance. I grabbed the moribund herb and stuck it in the nearest bit of soil. To our amazement it turned a healthy green and began to thrive. Then last week Mrs H appeared triumphantly waving one of the many books she has which contain a plethora of helpful advice upon which she draws to steer Fortress H through the chicane of life.

This particular volume contained references to herbs. Under

the heading parsley was the following piece of information. "Parsley can be a difficult herb to grow although it is said to flourish in households where the woman is in charge."

Mrs H's piece of parsley is positively blooming. Presumably this demonstrates the extent to which she controls Fortress H.

Now, I know of a household where I wouldn't be at all surprised if there is a healthy crop of parsley. The male member has contacted me but requests anonymity. "Please refer to me only as 'A kindred spirit from North Norfolk' - I have my street cred to consider."

I shall call him Mr S and reveal no other details. No nothing. Not even that he lives in a village where there is a well-known shrine. Mr S makes the interesting observation that "'marriage' is the only word in the English language that is a sentence as well!"

He offers clear evidence of the parsley factor by admitting to the house rules to which he is subjected. Rule 1: Mrs S is always right. Rule 2: If she is wrong, Rule 1 applies.

Mr S writes also of what he describes as the "S" word. He is referring to the word "sorry" which so often seems to be missing form the female vocabulary. He says: "On the rare occasions that it is uttered by The Boss, it is mumbled sotto voce."

And he gets short shrift when he asks for confirmation of what he thought he heard. "I've said it once - I'm not repeating it!"

This set me thinking. When did Mrs H last say sorry to me? By sorry I mean when did she last apologise. She often says sorry but uses it in a completely different context.

"I'm sorry but you'll just have to sort your daughter out. I've had enough." That is not an apology. Sorry here means over to you chum, I've done my bit. No, I mean when did Mrs H last say to me: "I'm sorry Neil. I was in the wrong. And I shouldn't have shouted at you." Oh look, another airborne pig.

I think we need to get the weed killer out of the shed and apply house rule number 3. Nuke the parsley.

IMPATIENTLY WAITING IN THE DEPARTURE LOUNGE

All right I was grumpy, I admit it. But who wouldn't have been. It was Sunday, the sun was shining and Mrs H had decreed that the pull towards the common good would be suspended and the family could go out for the day.

When Mrs H cuts us some slack like this I shiver. Firstly it means an acrimonious couple of hours while we prepare for the off and secondly it heralds a spell of double time when we get back to "catch up with all those jobs that I just haven't got round to."

Once Mrs H had made the formal announcement that the shackles were to be removed the inmates of Fortress Haverson each seemed to be pulling in different directions. The Brats disappeared and Mrs H went into ball gown selection mode. As usual I was left to fill a flask and run up a sandwich or two. The only assistance I received was: "You have put some salad in haven't you? We need some goodness not just rubbish."

By the time I had finished there was still no sign of the younger inmates. I had heard their mother bawling at them to get ready and "make sure you put a jumper in." And Mrs H herself had travelled between bathroom and bedroom so often that I thought she was operating some form of park and ride service.

Having thrown together a gourmet picnic I sloped off to sort myself out. Naively I always labour under the illusion that, by the time I'm ready, the rest of 'em will be champing at the bit to go. Of course, it never works like this and sure enough, having been the last to get ready I was first at the car. This is the point at which I became more than a trifle tetchy. And, predictably, my hall pacing and key-jangling elicited a response from Mrs H.

"If you've nothing to do, hurry them along. And make sure they've got their coats." The Brats heard all this but I still had to hunt them out and repeat the orders.

"I've only got to change and I'm ready," announced Mrs H. This always sounds quite positive but in fact means we are still anything up to half an hour away from departure. Eventually, she appeared but we weren't ready to start the engine yet.

"Do you think I'll be warm enough in this top?"

"Yes, yes! You'll be fine. Can we go now?" I replied impatiently.

"Look. If you're going to be like this I'm not going. No, I mean it." In the interest of a quiet life I capitulated and I actually got to prompt the car engine into life. But my irritability returned as we went through those inevitable pre-flight checks. The "Have you closed the toilet window" inquisition. It was at this point that Mrs H proposed a solution to my grumpiness.

"Coo you aren't half grumpy sometimes!" she said. "You're getting old. We need to do more spontaneous things to keep you young." I enquired what sort of things she meant. "Well, if they're spontaneous I don't know do I, you prawn?"

"It wouldn't work anyway," I scoffed. "There's no such thing as a spontaneous event with you. You need two weeks notice to get ready." White knuckles gripping the steering wheel I braced myself for storm force winds. Instead she threw down the gauntlet.

"And when did you last suggest we do anything spontaneous?" she challenged. "Come on then. You can't think can you?" she bated me, capitalising on my silence. The machinations of my brain were almost audible as it strove desperately to produce an ace that would snatch victory from the jaws of defeat.

"I can't remember the last time because I gave up years ago because it's hopeless," I babbled petulantly. Mrs H just smiled. We travelled some miles before I felt able to become part of the Fortress social fabric again.

All this has inspired a campaign which Mrs H describes as "an attempt to modernise you". The targets are my appearance, my wardrobe and my behaviour. The younger inmates have started the ball rolling making radical suggestions for updating my hairstyle. Also, they inform me it is imperative that I wear jeans which carry a designer label and not my usual safe, comfy ones. And Brat Major made no attempt to hide her contempt when we met a friend in the street and I exchanged some banter with him.

"Oh Dad, you are so sad!"

With all this interest in my image, I feel a bit like a building about to be refurbished. They'll probably pin a notice on me saying: "Neil Haverson is closed for modernisation. We apologise for any inconvenience."

They better not push it too far or they may see me march out the front door with my suitcase and a quite different notice pinned on my back.

"Under New Management."

MRS H AND LETHAL WEAPON TOO!

The Fortress kitchen has witnessed some tense scenes, usually when a Sunday lunch is being prepared. But a couple of weeks ago I think we probably went the extra mile. I'm not sure whether to attribute the cause to the late night we had on the Saturday or the new potato peeler. In fact, it was probably a bit of both.

The trouble with the Saturday night was the film. It started very late in the evening. We decided to watch half of it then tape the rest. But you know how it is, once we got involved, we watched just a few more minutes then a few more and before we knew it there was only half an hour left. Oh what the heck, might as well see the end now.

The upshot of all this was that we were late up on the Sunday morning. With relatives due for Sunday lunch, time was not on our side. Mrs H banged around the house complaining constantly that she would never be ready and should have got up in the early hours. Lunch would be ruined. And how do other people manage?

It was the turn next for the peeler to play its ace. We have been meaning to get a new peeler for ages. The old one had parted company with the handle making it difficult to hold. It was past its peel-by date and could do no more than mutilate vegetables

Then Mrs H returned home with this lethal weapon. It is shaped like a large bottle opener and the idea is to drag it across the vegetable. It whips off the peel and anything else in its path, as Mrs H found out.

I was not in the room at the time but I was alerted by a single word bellowed venomously with a mixture of pain and anger. It echoed around Fortress H but thanks to closed windows and doors failed to reach the outside world.

Brat Major, who was on the phone to one of her mates, was heard to mutter: "My mum must have really hurt herself. She never uses that word." Brat Minor's ears were unsullied. Help in the kitchen had been requested so once again he had done his Lord Lucan and vanished.

I hastened to Mrs H's aid. She had chiselled a chunk out of her finger while peeling an apple for a dish called Apple Slump. No, don't ask, suffice it to say it complements the Aubergine Bake.

Snarling furiously, she disappeared to the bathroom to apply a plaster. "This is all I want. As if I wasn't far enough behind already." She returned to the kitchen. "You'll all have to help now. I can't manage it all with this cut in my thumb."

I was allocated to peeling. Bravely I seized the peeler and carefully dealt with the apples. Mrs H then attempted to construct the Apple Slump but her pastry had other ideas. It refused to roll out and disintegrated. I sensed that word might be uttered again but Brat Major came to the rescue.

"I'll make some more pastry," she said scornfully. "My pastry's better than yours anyway." Mrs H stood back gratefully but after a few minutes felt obliged to question her daughter's recipe. Instead of making pastry, Brat Major was busy preparing a scone mixture.

Having come out unscathed from dealing with the apples I turned my attention to the potatoes. I moved on to the carrots and then the parsnips completing the job with only one small laceration to the little finger.

You may think I was flying solo here but in fact Mrs H was barking orders throughout. Unfortunately I was concentrating so hard on peeling without losing any appendages that I failed to absorb the instructions for chopping the parsnips.

There had been some debate as to whether I should carve out the middles in case they were "woody". I must have missed the command not to do this because I hacked merrily away until Mrs H staged a spot inspection.

"I told you not cut the middles out!" she exclaimed. "Look how thin they are. When I roast them they'll be like chips." She was really motoring now. "And you haven't done enough carrots or potatoes for six of us. Oh this is a disaster! I wish I hadn't got up this morning."

"All right, all right," I replied testily. "I'll have less than anyone else to make up." What a martyr.

Eventually everything came together. I served myself frugal portions of vegetables and looked pitifully at everybody else's plate.

"Are we trying to make a point, dear?" enquired Mrs H sarcastically. Fortunately she didn't hear my mumbled reply. Nor did she hear Brat Major's observation on her mother's catering efforts that morning. It was a chilling warning whispered in my ear with an air of desperation.

"Dad! Do you realise it's Mum's turn to do Christmas Dinner for the family this year?"

WHAT'S FOR
DINNER DEAR?

An air of mystery usually surrounds evening meals at Fortress Haverson. Often I don't know what's being served up until it's on the plate. Even then it can take a few subtle questions to establish precisely what I'm eating.

And, as I've mentioned so many times, the timing of the food's arrival is another great poser. It can vary anything up to three hours. Relatives never know when to telephone us in the evening. We always seem to end up spitting food down the 'phone and telling them we'll ring them back just as soon as we've finished eating.

Imagine, therefore, my surprise when one night Mrs H gave 24 hours notice of the following evening's dinner menu. It came about because she was planning something the children refuse to eat so she was after me to cough up some dinner money for them.

It was a strange feeling going to work equipped with the knowledge of what awaited my homecoming. But just what was this mouth-watering dish, a dish that had sparked rebellion in the Brats? Yes, you've guessed. It was the celebrated Aubergine Bake.

When I got home there was no sign of activity in the kitchen so I headed for the bedroom to change. Bravely I picked up a book and began reading. Every now and again I slammed a drawer. It doesn't help me read, but I find it works well if I make a lot of noise because she thinks I am heavily engaged in doing something constructive.

Eventually hunger got the upper hand and I thought it time to drop a hint or two. As I entered the kitchen Mrs H was gingerly extracting the aubergine from the fridge like a midwife delivering a baby.

"Ah," she said as I entered. "You can wash this for me." As if I was the proud mother she placed the aubergine reverently in my hands. I took it to the sink and gently bathed it. Then all ceremony was lost as Mrs H set about the hapless vegetable with a kitchen knife.

Every now and again a brat strayed into the kitchen and made derisory comments. This prompted me to ask Mrs H to explain exactly what the benefits of eating aubergine are. After all, most of our meals are accompanied by a short lecture on the goodness her fare provides.

For instance, she advocates broccoli because its vitamins are beneficial for the heart. Carrots appear regularly on our plates so we get a good shot of beta carotene to help fight cancer. But the aubergine remains a mystery.

For once Mrs H was stumped. However, she has a massive stock of reference books. If you get bitten by some unpronounceable reptile in the Amazon Jungle, just contact Mrs H. The chances are she can look up the antidote. She selected an appropriate volume from her library and invited me find the aubergine.

"Can't be essential part of our diet," I sneered. "It's not even in the index."

"Oh give it to me," she replied impatiently. "You won't find it under aubergine, it's called eggplant." Eggplant Bake. Doesn't have the same ring to it somehow does it? Mrs H flicked to the right page but then went silent.

"Oh," she said somewhat taken aback. "It says here that in Nigeria it is highly regarded as a contraceptive." I couldn't help wondering how it works. Does the female take a bite out of it each night. Or do they have the morning after aubergine?

"Ah , this is more like it," she said reading on. "It acts as an inhibitor, preventing build-up of certain things in the body." She went on to quote evidence that will surely have every reader rushing to the greengrocers. I suggest you place a regular order. Just consider this.

Rats given a seizure-producing drug and then fed on eggplant were found to be much less likely to have convulsions. Now that's interesting because I had been pretty close to a seizure when I discovered Brat Minor swinging out of his bedroom window trying to erect a radio aerial on the roof. Had the Aubergine Bake saved me? But wait, there's more.

An Austrian scientist fed rabbits a high cholesterol diet. Some he also gave doses of eggplant. It didn't say whether he served it diced with potatoes in a tomato sauce. However, in those rabbits fortunate enough to chomp some eggplant, the build up of fatty plaque was dramatically reduced. Pretty conclusive stuff eh?

Well, I pointed out to Mrs H that I do not come from Nigeria. Neither am I a convulsing rat nor an obese rabbit. I was about to demand that Aubergine Bake be removed from the Fortress menu when she read the final paragraph.

"In a Japanese population survey, eating eggplant was associated with an increased death rate." Come to think of it, I have got a bit of stomachache.

No, she wouldn't - would she?

TIRED OUT
AND SHATTERED

You know how it is when you've had a bad day. Your head feels as if someone has surgically inserted a roll of barbed wire, your shoulders are that rigid with tension you could double for an electricity pylon and your mouth tastes as though it has been recently coated with emulsion.

I arrived home from work the other evening with all these symptoms plus a few more. I was met by the younger inmates of Fortress Haverson who were in the drive talking to a friend. I returned their greetings with as amiable a grunt as I could muster. As I walked down the path a pleasant idea forced its way through the roll of barbed wire and projected welcoming images into my mind. A nice long, relaxing soak in a hot bath, that's what I needed.

It would take all my guile and cunning to get an addition to my hot water allowance let alone obtain clearance for a bath at such a peak time of frantic activity. As I approached the back door I could see Mrs H through the window.

I decided attack was the best defence. I burst through the door and, before she could get a word in, started talking. Having babbled a load of drivel to grab centre stage I finished up with a hasty: "Gorna 'ave a quick bath, OK?"

To my astonishment this was authorised. But little did I know that fate was in collusion with Mrs H and one of those unexpected incidents was about to occur which do so enhance life at Fortress H.

I had got as far as removing my jacket and tie and was enjoying the anticipation of wallowing in a steaming tub followed by the can of beer I had hidden at the back of the fridge. Suddenly, there was a commotion at the back door.

"Dad, Dad! Quick!" It was Brats Major and Minor both sporting expressions of startled excitement. "The car sunroof just shattered!" This was followed by statements designed to exonerate themselves from any form of blame. "We didn't touch it. We weren't anywhere near it. We didn't throw a stone or anything." They had even brought their mate with them as a witness for the defence.

I was escorted to the crime scene and shown the exact locations of the suspects when the event took place. The jagged glass, scattered around inside the car, twinkled in the fading light as if there had been a sharp hoarfrost. The drama was compounded when Mrs H revealed that the weather forecast was rain. The car had to go in the garage until it could be fixed.

A simple manoeuvre you might think. Not so. Apart from the slivers of glass likely to cause permanent damage to the driver, the summer months have seen such an accumulation of odds and ends put into "temporary" storage in the garage that it was in state rivalling Brat Minor's squat on a good day.

Old newspapers waiting to be taken to the recycling skip, boxes of jumble and goodness knows why I had abandoned the wheel barrow in there. Probably I had been gardening when Mrs H diverted me to other duties. Anyway, I had to find a home for it all.

At the end of the garage I have a worktop. The original purpose of this was to provide somewhere for me to practice my extremely limited skills as a handyman. In reality it has become a graveyard for my failed attempts at matters practical.

Aided by Brat Major, who had generously agreed to sacrifice doing homework to help me, I swept the bits of broken wood, bent metal and abandoned screws to one side and we loaded the surface with cardboard boxes. By the time we had finished, the unit was stacked precariously to the ceiling.

Risking lacerations to important parts of the body, I climbed gingerly into the car and drove into garage. A sheer escarpment of boxes confronted me. I made a mental note to warn Mrs H. I don't know who would suffer more, her or me if she slammed the car door and got buried under an avalanche?

The windscreen company I rang for help proved to be expert witnesses on behalf of the Brats. Apparently it is not uncommon for sunroofs to break, probably due to a weakness in the glass combined with a change in temperature. They also told me the price. Thank heaven for insurance. The sunroof alone was to cost £400!

This was a real eye-opener. Well, in Mrs H's case it was real mouth-opener. She was so stunned that her jaws parted to their maximum extent, a width normally reserved exclusively for verbal Haverson bashing.

I must say all this intense activity proved admiral therapy for removing the barbed wire from my head and releasing the tension from my shoulders. Mind you, given the choice, I'd plump for a nice hot bath.

PAINTING
BY NUMBERS

For years I have shouldered the burden of being the sole person to do any decorating at Fortress Haverson. I've dealt with this stressful responsibility by using every delaying tactic at my disposable. Suddenly things have changed and I can only assume that my procrastination was the cause of the unprecedented scenes of teamwork witnessed recently at Fortress H.

We have a small room in which the younger inmates kept all their books and games. Recently it's become the mog's dormitory. A while ago Mrs H decided this room should be decorated and turned into a sanctuary where studious brats could do homework and generally be neither seen nor heard.

I was then subjected to constant harassment designed to galvanise me into painting. Weeks went by and there was no sign of action. Then Brat Major joined the campaign. She became so enthusiastic that she offered to help. Eventually I cracked and Mrs H announced that I would be taking a couple of days off at half term and we would all pitch in.

On the first day of family painting Mrs H was away on a course but that still left three of us. Brat Major and I reported for duty but where was Lord Lucan? I went in search of Brat Minor and discovered him lurking in his squat. I enquired when he would be joining us. There followed a short speech, the gist of which was this.

Sadly, he had been unaware of the planned decorating. How it had not come to his attention over the past weeks while his mother had been nagging his father to do it, he just couldn't think. He had now arranged to play football with his chums so tragically he would not be available to assist. "Oh and if you're going to get some paint first perhaps you could drop me off at the park". In the end the lazy little toad never even set foot in the room.

Apart from bumping into each other occasionally, and arguing over which radio station to listen to, the Truculent Teenager and I got on quite well. By the time Mrs H arrived to inspect our work, the room had been totally cleared and the ceiling and woodwork painted.

While emptying the room we did stumble across one problem. Stashed behind a pile of games was a decomposing banana. Clearly it had come home in a lunch box and been hidden to avoid retribution from Mrs H.

Since Brat Major does not eat bananas - "They're disgusting!"- Lord Lucan was interviewed about this. He denied all knowledge, indicating that the perpetrator must be some distant relative of the tooth fairy.

Quite how Her Truculence and I achieved such productivity I do not know for when Mrs H took over as foreman the next morning it was clear that we had been rudderless. I soon discovered who was in charge when I challenged her authority.

"It'll take you ages to do that," I commented as she set about painting the wall. "You need a larger brush than that."

"No I don't. I like a small brush. I always use one this size," she rasped.

Next she questioned the thoroughness of our preparation. "I've found a cobweb. Did you wash the walls first? And just look at the radiator. Aren't you going to take it off the wall to paint behind it?"

Before I could answer Brat Major chimed in, pointing out that we would get on faster if her mother did less talking and more painting. Well, I knew there would be fireworks with her and Mrs H cooped up in a small room. It's like trying to put a fire out with petrol.

"Look, I'll go. I'll walk out." replied Mrs H with venom. "I've got plenty of other things to get on with." Whoops! Time to shut up. And so, we continued in silence. As they painted the edges I applied paint to the walls with the roller. Doing all this in a confined space was not easy. We may well have come up with a new Olympic sport. Synchronised painting.

To complete the room we bought some carpet. Mrs H measured it and directed me where to cut. As I sliced my way gingerly round the room, she bawled commands like a drill instructor.

"Knife blade up! Cut up, up up. Now straight, keep going, steady round the door! New blade." In my haste to change the blade I cut myself.

"Oh no!" cried Mrs H. "Keep your finger up. It's a new carpet, blood'll stain it. I'll never get it out." Thanks! Don't worry about me.

I used to find decorating therapeutic but that was when I was my own boss. Now, following this exhibition of Haverson cohesion, there is much talk of a combined assault on the hall and north wing. I'm not sure if I can handle it.

I wonder if Brat Minor would let me go to the park with him.

MRS H BAKES
EXCEEDINGLY GOOD TARTS

I don't usually make New Year's resolutions. Not because I don't keep them; that's academic. Mrs H makes them for me so it follows that failure to stick to them is not an option. However, this year I have decided to set myself a challenge or two.

It's time I put my foot down a bit and inserted a few cogs of my own into the wheels that drive the pull towards the common good at Fortress H. I'm going to have a bash at influencing what food turns up in the Fortress larder.

I know what you're thinking. Here he goes again, banging on about the Aubergine Bake. Well, you're wrong. It's not what gets served up but more a case of what doesn't. We all have the odd treat that leads us into temptation; usually fattening and thoroughly bad for you. Well I have three which, over the years, seem to have been phased from the Fortress menu.

Top of the absentee list is Bakewell tart followed closely by lemon meringue pie. Third spot goes to Yorkshire pudding though I do have to admit this does put in the odd appearance. I tend to forget about it because it is not always recognisable; especially when heavily disguised as Mrs H's version of toad in the hole.

I don't know why the other two have disappeared because Mrs H is quite capable of manufacturing them. In fact she turns out a particularly mean lemon meringue pie. Anyway, I wouldn't object if she bought them from a shop occasionally if it meant I could reacquaint my taste buds with a little bit of what I fancy.

We've passed bakers' shops and I've pressed my nose up against the window, soulful eyes gazing at the last Bakewell in the shop. Mrs H remains unmoved. It's either: "You have enough sweet things without stuffing yourself with pastry." Or: "I'm not spending good money on things like that when I can make them with twice the flavour for half the price."

When I point out that her skill at constructing Bakewell tart seems to have gone dormant, she retaliates with, "When do you think I get time to make things like that. Do you know, he's got glue all over his school shirt again? That's two shirts I've got to soak, wash, dry and iron before the morning or he'll have nothing to wear tomorrow. And you expect me to find time to make Bakewell tart?"

Of course it wasn't always like this. If I rummage in the

treasure chest of memories, I can recall a young wife, eager to please her new husband, pandering to the odd whim. My penchant then was for scampi, a dish Mrs H hadn't had. Mind you, I'm going back to the days when it was a real luxury to go to the pub and lash out on scampi in the basket.

Just married and living in a small flat, such an extravagance was beyond our means. But the youthful Mrs H thought she'd treat me. She invested some of our meagre earnings in some scampi and proceeded to deep-fry it. Maybe she got distracted. but I was served half a dozen or more small pieces of rock.

Manfully I sawed my way through the granite-like outer casing of breadcrumbs only to discover that most of the scampi had vanished. To this day I can still hear a disdainful Mrs H as she hacked away at her portion. "I'm not very impressed with scampi."

"It's not supposed to be like this," I said tactfully. In those days I was brave enough to make such comments, these days I leave it to the younger inmates. The worst of it was, the memory of the aborted meal lingered for days as it was impossible to expel the aroma of intense deep-frying from our tiny abode.

Thankfully, Mrs H's culinary skills have developed over the years and she is now in a class where, as you well know, there is little she cannot do with an aubergine. Sadly not much of her expertise has rubbed off on me so the chances of me producing my own Bakewell Tart are slim.

Delving into the memory bank to turn up exploits of a younger Mrs H has reminded me that she has requested me to set the record straight on a small matter. Brat Minor has been telling his friends that his mother is 56 years old. What is worse, he wasn't joking; he really thought she was.

Mrs H, who I must say looks pretty good for her age, was aghast and pointed out to her son that she would probably be of interest to medical science if she was in fact 56.

A mixture of loyalty and fear prevent me revealing Mrs H's actual age. After all, I still harbour faint hopes that one day I will open the cake tin to be greeted by you know what.

THE SOUNDS
OF CHRISTMAS

Fortress H is a noisy place to live. Mind you, I have got used to most of the din that goes on. In fact, it wouldn't seem right lying in bed listening to Mrs H giving the day's closing headlines without the washing machine rumbling away in the background. It's like having a bedroom above an underground station.

Having finally got to sleep, it seems no time at all before I am woken by a dawn chorus courtesy of the gas boiler. As soon as the timer fires it into life the house is serenaded with a series of boings and bangs that sound like a Caribbean steel band warming up. This inspires an ensemble of gurgling radiators to join in as they receive their first fix of hot water for the day.

And to ensure that sleep is no longer an option for me a Brat will rise to do the homework it should have done the night before. This activity cannot be carried out without slamming a good few doors, loud fussing of the mog and pouring of Cornflakes into a bowl with a noise like a lorry unloading gravel.

There's no respite when I get up. Throughout the day Fortress H will echo to the bloodcurdling yells of battling Brats indulging in sibling rivalry. There is always a hi fi somewhere playing at full belt - usually to an empty room. And of course the rallying cries of Mrs H driving us ever onward are an essential ingredient of Fortress life.

Me? Well, you rarely hear a peep from me. I may raise my voice occasionally at the younger inmates and I did once shout at Mrs H. But that was only because she couldn't hear me over her Jools Holland CD.

I mention all this because Christmas saw the introduction of a couple of noise-producing items that have added to the racket. Mrs H was given this musical coffee mug. Stand it on the table it remains silent. Pick it up and you are treated to a rendition of Jingle Bells. The workings are recessed into the underside of the mug. Or rather, they were.

Unfortunately the bottom fell out. The mug is perfectly useable but the musical bit was abandoned in the kitchen. For days it sat there minding its own business, then suddenly it took to bursting into life in response to certain sounds.

We'd switch on the light and away it would go. Spreading butter on toast was enough to galvanise it into action. Even flinging open the roller blind produced a chorus of Yuletide music. No matter what we did, shake it, bang it on the table, Mrs H even shouted at it, it refused to stop until it had exhausted its full repertoire.

Finally Mrs H cracked and hurled it in the bin. A last refrain of Jingle Bells was heard from the depths of the bin bag as it was carted out for the dustmen.

As if this wasn't enough, Brat Minor got one of those key rings that bleeps. You know the type, if you lose it, all you have to do is whistle and it trills its whereabouts. Well, we have discovered this excitable bit of gubbins can't wait to twitter - and not just at the sound of a whistle.

A cough will do it; even normal conversation will produce a chirp. And we think it's fallen in love with the telephone. It responds to each ring of the phone with a seductive warble as if it's answering a mating call.

It likes the television too. A good car chase is usually accompanied by a series of rapid bleeps that sound like a budgerigar with its foot trapped in the cage door.

Watching television can be a noisy activity anyway at Fortress H, especially when Mrs H washes her hair. She has the happy knack of arriving at the drying stage just as the programme is reaching its climax.

She shuffles close to the set, cranks up the volume and switches on the hairdryer. There we sit for a good 15 minutes, straining to pick up the odd word of the plot. I daren't complain because I get chapter and verse as to why she hasn't done it earlier.

"Well, when do you think I should have done it? I had to do dinner then she wanted some help with her maths. Then I had to wash the school trousers he wore today because the stain still hasn't come out of the other pair. I had to do my shopping list for the supermarket tomorrow. Oh and GBH rang." Ah, now things are becoming clear. "You'll never guess what she told me..."

And the more excited she gets the more that wretched key ring bleeps. She only has to open her mouth and it responds. Come to think of it, she has much the same affect on me.

GREAT LENGTHS
FOR A PAIR OF TROUSERS

I know children aren't all the same shape and size. And I'm sure manufacturers do their best when they label clothes with such things as "Fits 12 years". But Brat Minor seems to be of such dimensions that he pinches a measurement from around 3 age groups.

Mrs H has searched the city to find him a pair of trousers for school. We need at least three pairs because at any one time two of them are always in the wash. Goodness knows what he gets up to but he comes home with unidentifiable stains that resist even Mrs H's best efforts to remove.

He has been surviving with just the two pairs for ages. Mrs H went to the usual store for a new pair but they didn't have the same make as his others. She managed to buy a pair that were identical in style and marked for the right age and size but when he tried them on they were two inches longer.

"You'll have to change them in your lunch hour," Mrs H informed me. I touched forelock dutifully and asked for detailed instructions. After all, if the great lady herself couldn't find the right fit how did she expect me to crack it?

"Right, listen carefully," she said. "First make sure this pair haven't got the wrong label in. Find an identical pair, put them together and measure them. If they're the same length you'll have to try a smaller size but make sure the waist is big enough. If you get stuck ask an assistant."

I wandered round all the racks of boys' trousers but couldn't find anything similar. I turned on my pathetic spouse look and asked an assistant. She took one look at me and said: "Oh you need to speak to Ruth." Is this a new service? Do stores now have a member of staff specially trained to deal with inept husbands?

Ruth went straight to a rack of identical trousers. Confirmed they were marked correctly and that the next size down would be far too small. "Oh dear," I stammered. Then I came to a bold decision. "I'd better hang on to these and ask my wife what she wants to do." Ruth smiled knowingly and I fled.

I reported back to Mrs H and was told that I would be returning to the store the next day to get a refund.

The following day, just before I went to lunch, the phone rang. It was Mrs H. "I'm coming into the city," she announced. "I'll meet you inside the shop at the boys wear about half past one. I want to have a look at these trousers."

I was there at the appointed time, Mrs H wasn't. I pretended to know what I was about, carefully studying all manner of boys trousers until I thought I must be arousing suspicion. I felt that every security camera in the vicinity must be trained on me.

I decided to wait at the entrance to the store. There I stood for a good ten minutes. Eventually I gave up and went back to work. When I arrived home that evening I charged Mrs H with failing to appear on time.

"I was there," she protested vehemently. "I hung around until they must have thought I was a shop lifter then I gave up and went to look at the women's clothes."

"But," I protested, "I waited outside the shop for ages and I didn't see you go in."

"No you wouldn't," she explained nonchalantly. "I went in the rear entrance." I expressed as much annoyance as I dare while she seemed to find it all rather amusing.

I managed to avoid all mention of children's clothes for the next week. Then I came home one Saturday evening to be greeted by an excited Brat Major.

"I'll show you the skirt I bought today," she said. As she rushed up stairs to get it, Mrs H hissed a warning to me out of the corner of her mouth, "Tell her she's not wearing it out."

I had to agree. Brat Major appeared with what I can only describe as a thin black net curtain. I made stern fatherly statements - with a hint of sarcasm.

"I hope it wasn't expensive because it would be a shame to pay a lot for something you're only going to wear around the house. You're certainly not going out in that!" There were the usual comments that everybody is wearing them and what a "sad person" I am. Then came the killer blow.

"Well, if you won't let me wear it you can take it back." Oh no. I'll have a go at boy's trousers but a girl's skirt? No way, especially this one. Mrs H came to my rescue.

"I'm going shopping on Monday. I'll change it." Thank you dear. You..er...don't want me to meet you do you?

TRY THE BIN -
BUT WHICH ONE

When Mrs H gets exasperated, which I have to say is quite often, she relieves her frustration by letting fly a penetrating "Arrgghh!" It reminds me of those peacocks that strut around the gardens of stately homes shrieking at visitors.

I was absorbed in my duties in the kitchen one Saturday evening when I was rudely awoken by a screech from the Fortress peacock. I turned to see Mrs H sporting an anguished expression and waving a letter.

"I searched everywhere for this today," she exploded. "I even emptied the bin thinking I'd thrown it away and it was here all the time." She had discovered it where she files all her current paperwork, in a heap on top of the breadbin. She proceeded to give me a colourful blow by blow account of picking her way through the rubbish.

Later that evening Brat Major appeared to demand if I had speculated the Fortress finances on the Lottery. I replied that I had and the ticket was, yes, on the breadbin. After a search Brat Major announced that it wasn't there.

"Arrgghh!" the peacock interjected. "I thought it was last week's and threw it in the bin. Don't say I've got to go through that lot again."

"It's up to you if you want to leave several million pounds lying in the bin," I replied smugly. With a noise that sounded as though one of those visitors had finally strangled the peacock, she donned the Marigolds and reacquainted herself with the contents of the bin.

The missing lottery ticket, somewhat soggy and now embellished with a variety of substances, was found and left to lie in state on the floor until the numbers were checked.

I know what you're thinking, this was some kind of omen. Having disposed of the lottery ticket, it was rescued in the nick of time and made the Haversons so rich they could afford a stately home, complete with peacocks.

Well, out of two lines we got just one number that matched those drawn. So Fortress H remains financially challenged and Mrs H has plenty to go Arrgghh! about.

I must admit the peacock impression does seem to work for Mrs H where as it doesn't for me. I developed a cold the other week and went through all the misery of sore throat, persistent cough and nose running like a tap. On a number of occasions I responded to a outbreak of sneezing with an attempted Arrgghh! but achieved no more than inducing a further bout of coughing.

I fought the cold as long as I could before giving in. I staggered in to work where, throughout the day that nice chap I share an office with issued regular bulletins on the development of his own symptoms, clearly apportioning blame should he be smitten. Eventually I took the hint and went home.

I arrived at a deserted Fortress H around twenty past three. I was just contemplating bed when the back door was thrown open and two schoolbags hurtled through it followed by two boisterous Brats high on energy generated by their release from the constraints of academia.

"Ah," said Brat Major. "Glad you're here, we've got an appointment at the hairdressers at 4 o'clock. You can take us in the car." Like a fool I did.

I arrived home ripe for slipping between the sheets but before I could undo my shoe laces Mrs H walked in.

"Thought you'd be in bed," she said and then proceeded to delay my departure by recounting a couple of adventures she had had that day. I finally made it to kip sometime after 5 o'clock.

I arose about 7.15 p.m. and had some tea. It was at this point that Mrs H made what was the biggest gesture of sympathy I had received all day.

"I'll help you wash up," she said generously. For an inmate of Fortress H to offer to help me wash up is clear recognition that I am unwell. Then the phone went; it was for Mrs H. And wouldn't you know it, her call concluded at precisely the same time as I completed the washing up.

I headed back to bed at around half past ten. Mrs H thought she may as well have an early night too so instead of getting off to sleep quickly, I had to listen to the closing headlines as usual. Finally the day's news was imparted, I slapped soothing cream on my red nose, gulped some cough linctus and was about to squeeze some gunge up my nose to help me breathe when Mrs H barked at me.

"You need to be careful with that!" she exclaimed. "It's got Ephedrine in it." I enquired what danger this posed me. "Well, I wasn't allowed to have it when I was pregnant." There was only one answer to that.

Arrgghh!

PARENTS ARE
OFF THE AGENDA

The times they are a changing. It seems that gone are the days when Mrs H or I could make a pronouncement on something such as a family outing and it would happen. 'Tis true, the younger inmates of Fortress H would have a good whinge but there was never any doubt that they would toe the line. Now, all of a sudden, the lure of more interesting things and their desire to exploit their increasing independence is triumphing over their boring parents.

I had a day off at half term, during that spell of exceptionally mild and sunny weather. It seemed to me a must that we seized the opportunity to go out. First plans had to be submitted to Mrs H for authorisation. "Tell you what," I said, "let's go to the coast when I'm off."

"You better sort it out with your children," she said mysteriously. I noticed she had relinquished her share in the ownership with the phrase "your children". This meant there was a problem. I sought out the younger inmates and managed to capture some of their attention from the television.

"Hey," I said with boyish enthusiasm, "thought we might go to the sea on my day off." Now, when they were small this would have been greeted with whoops of delight. More latterly their restrained response belied the pleasure in their eyes. But this time I was presented with two faces sporting looks of something approaching utter bewilderment.

"The sea? Why would we want to go there?" enquired a puzzled Brat Minor. "What would we do?" Then he revealed the real reason as he added pompously, "Besides, I've already got plans."

"And I'm going into the city shopping," added his sister. I turned to leave the room with such a look of disappointment that Brat Minor mellowed slightly.

"I could be free by about 4 o'clock if you really want to go out," he said in a business-like way. I pointed out that by the time we got to the beach it would be virtually dark but by this time they had committed their full attention back to the television.

I reported to Mrs H who showed no surprise. She pointed out they now have their own agendas which don't include tedious parents.

It transpired that Brat Minor and a mate had arranged to

meet a couple of friends in the village. It emerged that these friends were both girls. Had he not heeded any of my warnings? Already a member of the opposite sex was coming between him and a day at the beach. Where would it end?

I knew it was serious when my day off dawned and I got up to find the young man washing his hair! He has not carried out this act of personal hygiene voluntarily for as long as I can remember. Normally it takes several days of haranguing by Mrs H before he will acknowledge that his lank mop needs to liase with the shampoo.

I peered through the bathroom door at this phenomenon. He grinned through steam heavily laced with something sweet he had sprayed liberally over his body. I decided to make no comment but to store this incident for future use.

He and his mate swaggered off to keep their assignation. I felt cheated. It was a superb day, warm with wall-to-wall sunshine and I was spending it doing the garden. I moaned to Mrs H continually, so much so that she eventually suggested we try again the following day.

First I established that the social calendars of both the young stop-outs were vacant before announcing that the Haversons would be heading for the countryside the following day. It was like old times. Immediately they laid down their conditions for accompanying us.

"We're not going to do a walk!" asserted Brat Major. Other provisos included certain concessions being granted throughout the rest of half term. These ranged from financial inducements to the further relaxing of the strict parental controls which they claim continually embarrass them with their friends.

The day itself slipped into the usual mould. Both of them protested that they were far too exhausted to walk so we plied them with chocolate. Most of the way round the way marked track they whined at the distance they were being made to cover so we gave politician's answers about how far we were from base. But when we completed the circuit ice creams had to be purchased to acknowledge the great sacrifice they had made in coming with us.

Then Brat Minor, discovered hidden depths of energy and produced his football. As I kicked around with him I recalled his preparations for meeting his young lady. Perhaps I should take a leaf out of his book. If I were to wash my hair at a strange time of day and plaster myself with a generous amount of body spray, it just might keep Mrs H on her toes.

GOOD EVENING,
HERE IS THE NEWS

Do you know, I can't remember the last time I came home from work and there was no Mrs H to greet me. This staggering fact hit me when, one evening recently, I bounced off the locked back door of a very silent Fortress H. Lights were on, indicating that someone was in residence but the absence of Mrs H's authoritative tones wafting through the evening air indicated she was out. This meant the younger inmates were most probably perpetrating deeds which are not permitted when their mother is at home.

I tried to gain access but I couldn't get my key in the lock; one was already in the other side. It was the same story at the front door. I hammered frantically on both doors and it took some persistence to prise a Brat away from its illegal doings. Eventually Brat Major came to my rescue.

"What were you up to?" I enquired.

While I may have hoped for an answer such as "I was engrossed in my homework", the response of "Oh, er...nothing" confirmed she was up to no good. I suspect she was watching something she shouldn't on television such as a late night film that we had recorded or, more likely, raiding the Fortress larder.

Brat Minor appeared at the top of the stairs blinked at me then disappeared into his squat, slamming the door. This sent me a clear "Do not disturb" message. I enquired as to the whereabouts of Mrs H and winced on being informed that she had gone for a wallet-emptying session at the supermarket.

Brat Major slunk away leaving me standing alone in the hall. I stood there for what seemed like an eternity. It was all so strange. Usually my entrance is like a switch; it triggers Mrs H into delivering the early evening news. I get no further than a few steps into the kitchen before she is belting out the headlines.

"The man didn't ring about the bathroom, the Visa bill's arrived and I dropped the jumble off at the village hall." Next follows the extended reports on any of these items that developed into a Mrs H adventure. Then we get the Trevor Macdonald "And finally" bit.

"You'll never guess what I did at work today! I wiped everything off the floppy disk on my computer. Well I didn't know what to do so I..." and so it goes on.

I don't mind this update but it can be frustrating if I am

bursting with news of my own and I have to wait until she finally pauses for breath so I can dive in. Even worse is when I am bursting with something else - the need to go to the loo. Believe you me, it is no mean feat grappling with an oversubscribed bladder while trying to appear riveted by Mrs H's every word.

But this night was different. The silence was uncanny. I went upstairs to change but when I got back downstairs I drifted rudderless around the house. You see, once Mrs H has caught me up with the day's events I usually receive my orders for the evening. Well, when I say orders, they're not always dispensed as instructions but often delivered with a "could you just do" type of phrase, to soften the blow that is being delivered.

"I thought you might like to drain the central heating system tonight." And the one that I always feel contains a hint of sarcasm: "I don't suppose it would be possible for you to clear all that stuff you've dumped beside the bed would it? If it's still there tomorrow I'm going to dump the lot."

Anyway, I made my way to the North Wing and picked up the paper which a Brat had left open at the television page. I noticed Star Trek was on. For one rash moment I found myself heading to turn on the set. Fortunately my pre-programming kicked in and I withdrew my hand as if I'd been stung. Phew that was close! Suppose Mrs H had walked past the window and spotted me watching television at 6 o'clock in the evening!

I was just beginning to panic when the door burst open and Mrs H appeared laden with shopping. "I don't suppose it would be possible for you to help me unload the car would it?" Eagerly I followed her down the path. At last I felt secure.

Soon after this there followed an incident, which demonstrated just how well, I've been pre-programmed. Poor old Mrs H had a cold and was having trouble sleeping. It transpired that I was not helping matters.

"You were really restless last night," she berated me. "You kept jiffling around all over the place. Eventually I got fed up and shouted 'Will you keep still!' You didn't wake up but it worked; you stopped." Scary!

It's a good job she didn't know what I was dreaming about.

SIGNING
MY LIFE AWAY

I arrived home the other evening at the same time as Mrs H. We exchanged greetings then walked silently down the path together. When we reached the back door, Mrs H wheeled round and fired with both barrels.

"Do you know, I was really put out today," she exploded. "When I came home at lunch time they said on the radio that it would rain. Look at it now; it's been dry all afternoon." Then came the climax to this speech. "And I didn't put my washing out!"

Well, what could a chap say? I put on my best mortified look and made appropriate noises to convey my devastation at this cruel meteorological blow which fate had dealt Mrs H. Mentally I retraced my day but I could come up with nothing remotely catastrophic to compete with this.

I thought no more about this until a few days later when Mrs H was preparing the evening meal. I glanced at the clock and, to my astonishment noted that we were still in the first half of the evening. All the signs were that my stomach could be in for a surprise with an early filling.

I spotted leeks and broccoli loitering on a chopping board so I knew we were in for one of Mrs H's healthy dishes. The upside was that there was no sign of an aubergine.

I managed to escape from the kitchen without being pressed into service. From a safe distance I listened to the sounds of chopping, sizzling and stirring. I was summoned occasionally to do the odd bit of washing up but generally I got off lightly.

Finally Mrs H announced that the meal was but a few minutes from being served. I was getting out the eating irons when a giggling Mrs H suddenly appeared.

"Guess what?" she chuckled. "I've forgotten to do the potatoes!" Driven by an empty stomach my answer was immediate.

"I'll go without," I insisted. "I am not waiting while you do potatoes. Gimme bread, gimme anything instead but I want my food!" Gosh I'm so assertive when I'm hungry.

"Do you know, that's the first time I've ever done that," mused Mrs H. Either, for once, I got my own way or Mrs H was hungry too for we ate a potato-less dinner.

Later that night I was reading the newspaper. Now, if it hadn't been for those two incidents, I probably wouldn't have paid as much attention as I did to the article on prenuptial agreements. Of course, this buzz phrase wasn't in existence when Mrs H trapped me. We put our names to the traditional agreement; for richer for poorer, in sickness and in health and all that.

But had I known what I know now, prior to the attachment of the ball and chain I may well have drawn up a document, detailing a few safeguards. Here are a few sample clauses:

Either party may conclude a conversation if they find it irrelevant and of no interest. For example, detailed descriptions of the trip round the supermarket giving up-to-date prices ("you should have seen how sprouts of shot up since last week") may be terminated with: "I'm going to clean the car".

As the car is driven by both parties, it is perfectly acceptable for either to insert petrol, oil and water. Cleaning of said car should be done as soon as it is dirty not left to see who cracks first.

It should not be assumed that just one of the parties will be responsible for the washing up. It is not obligatory to make phone calls immediately after meals, you know.

Either party may do the garden. Access to the shed is unlimited and there is no restriction on who may operate the lawnmower or perform the ancient skills of digging and weeding.

There is nothing to say that the party who chooses the paint for the walls shall play no part in applying it.

Responses to such questions as "What do you think of my new skirt?" shall be taken at face value and not assumed to have a hidden meaning like: "You're just saying that to shut me up".

Failure to return from the pub at the declared time is not sufficient grounds for the party left at home ironing to refuse to communicate in anything other than Neanderthal grunts.

Unfortunately I am closing the stable door when the horse has long since bolted. I learnt very early on in our married life that Mrs H had already drawn up her own prenuptial agreement.

Mind you, it's not the actual agreement I have trouble with; it's all the penalty clauses.

Also by the same author from the
Eastern Daily Press Classics series:

Fortress H: The Early years

Fortress H: The Aubergine Bake Repeats

Available from all good bookshops